The Business of Doing Good

Praise for this book

'This is an uplifting, hugely insightful read with key lessons for all of us. How to deliver societal as well as economic value is a challenge faced by big business, social enterprise and voluntary sector organizations like Concern and Oxfam alike. The blurring of our organizational boundaries has led to exciting innovation in this space that we all need to analyse more... It's a story of learning, innovation, resilience and the simplicity and importance we often forget of people connecting with people. Organizations like Oxfam support and learn from many local partner organizations like AMK. We all share the ambition that local organizations will become self-sustaining, dynamic contributors to overcoming poverty at national scale in poorer countries, but there are very few success stories of social enterprise at scale. Here is one.'

Penny Lawrence, Deputy Chief Executive,
Oxfam GB

'For funders, investors and donors, *The Business of Doing Good* is a must-read. In its granular portrayal of a value-laden, client-focused microfinance institution, the book asks us to re-evaluate and re-dedicate ourselves to designing funding mechanisms that strategically favor and fund the social enterprises which love their clients first and care for their investors second. This book calls us to be the kind of engaged, thoughtful, mission-focused bankers, accountants, investors, lawyers, analysts and auditors the world deserves.'

Jonathan C. Lewis, Founder/Chair,
MCE Social Capital

'A lucid and thought-provoking account of how things actually work in the field, based on the history and experience of AMK in Cambodia. It should become a well-thumbed staple for many of us working in social investment generally and microfinance especially.'

David Woods, Managing Director,
Oikocredit International

'Anyone who thinks too much of the discussion about social impact is theoretical – READ THIS!'

Tris Lumley, Director of Development,
New Philanthropy Capital & Co-chair G7 Social Impact Investment Taskforce

'The story of how something happens is endlessly fascinating to restless change agents. In this important new book, readers have the opportunity to dive deep into a successful social enterprise and distil important lessons for a range of future impact investments.'

Susan Davis, President & CEO,
BRAC USA

'Anton Simanowitz and Katherine Knotts have made an important and practical contribution to the discussion about how social enterprise and inclusive business can be more client-centered and contribute the most to the battle to end global poverty by 2030. By rigorously focusing on the critical issues related to client-centricity in a microfinance institution that has been off the radar of many industry observers, they provide a fresh and practical guide that will shape theory and practice for years to come.'

Alex Counts, President,
Grameen Foundation

'Based on the journey of one remarkable institution, the authors of *The Business of Doing Good* suggest six lessons on how to align an entire organization behind its social value aspirations. These lessons are a worthwhile read for anyone interested in what organizations need to do to sustainably improve the well-being of poor families in the context of market-based development.'

Tilman Ehrbeck, CEO
Consultative Group to Assist the Poor

'Simanowitz and Knotts have produced a comprehensive and highly readable chronicle of AMK's successful quest for growth combining financial viability with social relevance. It is not only an important document for microfinance sceptics as well as supporters but also for the growing numbers of people with an interest in social business; investments that support the lives of the under-privileged while generating acceptable returns for investors.'

Sanjay Sinha, Managing Director,
Microcredit Ratings International (M-Cril)

The Business of Doing Good
Insights from one social enterprise's journey to deliver on good intentions

Anton Simanowitz and Katherine E. Knotts

PRACTICAL ACTION
Publishing

Practical Action Publishing Ltd
The Schumacher Centre
Bourton on Dunsmore, Rugby,
Warwickshire CV23 9QZ, UK
www.practicalactionpublishing.org

ISBN 978-1-85339-864-3 Hardback
ISBN 978-1-85339-865-0 Paperback
ISBN 978-1-78044-864-0 Library Ebook
ISBN 978-1-78044-865-7 Ebook

Simanowitz, A., and Knotts, K., (2015) *The Business of Doing Good*,
Rugby, UK: Practical Action Publishing.
<http://dx.doi.org/10.3362/9781780448640>

Since 1974, Practical Action Publishing has published and disseminated
books and information in support of international development work
throughout the world. Practical Action Publishing is a trading name of
Practical Action Publishing Ltd (Company Reg. No. 1159018), the wholly
owned publishing company of Practical Action. Practical Action Publishing
trades only in support of its parent charity objectives and any profits
are covenanted back to Practical Action (Charity Reg. No. 247257,
Group VAT Registration No. 880 9924 76).

Cover design by Mercer Design
Indexed by Liz Fawcett
Typeset by Allzone Digital Services Limited
Printed by Replika Press Pvt. Ltd., India

Contents

http://dx.doi.org/10.3362/ 9781780448640.000

About the authors

Anton Simanowitz has been influential since the late 1990s as a practitioner and thought leader in the field of microfinance and social enterprise. He works globally with practitioners, investors, technical assistance providers and policy makers to improve the effectiveness of microfinance and social enterprises in delivering positive social outcomes.

Anton was founder and Director of the *Imp-Act* Consortium, a group of 12 leading microfinance organizations instrumental in the development of the Universal Standards in Social Performance management – industry standards in microfinance that are now widely used in due diligence, social audit, social rating, technical assistance and reporting. Most recently he led the design and roll-out to ten countries of a social performance diagnostic and capacity building approach for Dutch social investor Oikocredit.

His in-depth practical experience was gained working for five years as Chief Development Officer for the Small Enterprise Foundation, a globally recognised poverty-focused microfinance organization in South Africa, where he spearheaded efforts to re-engineer products and services and develop operational performance and quality control systems that integrate the organization's social and financial priorities.

Anton's work has included technical support and training to organizations in some 20 countries in the fields of social performance management, client monitoring systems, impact assessment, and poverty assessment. Anton has also supported a number of other international organizations such as the World Bank, the International Fund for Agricultural Development (IFAD), Hivos, Vision Fund, Save the Children, Plan International, the European Bank for Reconstruction and Development (EBRD) Coutts Bank, Big Society Capital, Toynbee Hall, Grameen Foundation, and the Ford Foundation.

He holds an honours degree from the University of Liverpool and a Masters in Development Economics from the University of East Anglia.

Katherine E. Knotts has worked with microfinance and other social purpose organizations for over 12 years to help them be better learners and communicators. As a writer, she focuses on helping organizations to analyse what's working (and what's not), distil lessons learned, and package those lessons for other practitioners through written and film media. She has published a range of thematic case studies for the MFC, Oikocredit, Habitat for Humanity and others, focusing on social performance management, financial education, client protection and housing microfinance.

On the strategic communications side, Katherine helps organizations tell their stories, design and create participatory learning spaces, and monitor the effectiveness of their advocacy initiatives. She is currently leading the strategic communications brief for the Microfinance Centre (MFC) Network, supporting the International Social Performance Task Force on their project communications efforts, and consulting for a range of other microfinance associations and investors. She was previously the Learning and Communications Manager for the *Imp-Act* Consortium, a group of 12 organizations providing thought- and practice-leadership on the global social performance management agenda.

As a trainer, she has designed and delivered a range of courses on strategic communications, social media and social performance management. Recently, she created the learning design templates for a new national financial education curriculum for the government of Uzbekistan.

Outside of the microfinance sphere, she has provided strategic communications support to Diverse City, a group of cultural entrepreneurs working for social change through the performing arts.

She is a graduate of Drew University (USA) and the London School of Economics (UK).

Preface

This book charts the evolution of Angkor Mikroheranhvatho (Kampuchea) Co. Ltd (AMK), a Cambodian microfinance organization, and its efforts to build an organizational business model to effectively serve hundreds of thousands of poor people in ways that bring tangible benefits to their lives. It is also the result of over 15 years of our own work in trying to analyse and advance the practice of microfinance and other social purpose organizations, to help them fully achieve their ambitions to reach and create value for poor and excluded people the world over.

We were commissioned by AMK to write a historical book based on the experience of the organization, partly in recognition of its 10th anniversary. As we immersed ourselves in AMK's story, our vision expanded as we recognized the value of this story to the wider world. This moved us away from a pure narrative history of AMK towards a book that explores the evolution of the organization, and the drivers of its decisions, successes, and failures. Our objective is to present an analysis that is accessible (and inspirational) to a broader audience interested in how to build organizations to deliver good, rather than one which appeals to microfinance practitioners alone.

The product then, is our interpretation of AMK. It is not a history, although it does tell the history of the organization. Rather than a chronological account of its development, we present insights emerging from our analysis of how AMK has evolved in the 11 years since its registration and, to some extent, from its 13 years of pre-history as a project of the international charity Concern Worldwide. As such, the analysis and conclusions are ours alone. While AMK funded the writing of the book, and has had input into its development, we have maintained full editorial control over the content. Any questions linked to factual errors, inaccuracies, controversial views or conclusions should be aimed towards us – the authors – rather than AMK.

Acknowledgements

The journey we have taken in writing this book can be measured in many ways. We have analysed more than 1,000 pages of internal documents and external evaluations, and have conducted over 100 hours' worth of interviews with AMK's Board members, current and former staff, clients, and investors. We have also talked to countless others, in Cambodia and elsewhere, who have either a connection to AMK or a perspective on Cambodia, microfinance, or the broader social enterprise sector. The process has been both enlightening and enjoyable; we have gained an insight into both AMK as an organization and the people who have devoted their energy to its work. Their commitment to the communities it serves was striking.

We are therefore deeply grateful for the time, support and patience of the following people.

Our external review panel. This helped shape the broad outline of the book, provided input and advice during the writing process, and gave detailed feedback on our first draft. These individuals were also formally named as an advisory group, established to mediate in the case of an editorial dispute between the authors and AMK. Fortunately no such dispute arose. They are: Lisa Kuhn-Frailoi, Independent Consultant (former Head of Latin America, Freedom from Hunger); Sanjay Sinha, Managing Director, Microfinance Credit Rating International Limited (India); and Joshua Morris, Managing Director, Emerging Markets Investments Pte Ltd (Cambodia).

Current and former AMK Board members, Chief Executive Officers and staff of Concern Worldwide. Gerhard Bruckermann; Tanmay Chetan; Howard Dalzell; Theresa McDonnell Friström; Tom O'Higgins; Jim Hynes; Irina Ignatieva; Tip Janvibol; Isabelle Kidney; Paul Luchtenburg; Rebecca McKenzie; Dina Pons; Pete Power; Frances Sinha; and Louise Supple.

Current and former AMK Management staff. Kea Borann, CEO; Prem Chandraboth, Head of Information Technology Department; Mam Choeurn, Chief Operations Officer; Nang Kinal, Head of Marketing Department; Peaing Pisak, Head of Human Resources; Suon Pisey, Head of Credit Operations Department; Chea Roattana, Head of Deposit & E-banking Department; Huot Sokha, Chief Business Officer; Pum Sophy, Head of Research Department; Chheang Taing, Chief Financial Officer; Le Theeda, former Head of Human Resources; Olga Torres, former Head of Research Department.

Other current and former AMK Head Office and Operations staff. When we visited AMK, we sought out staff who had been with AMK for a significant amount of time, to tap into their insights about how the organization developed over the years. We interviewed cleaners, drivers, branch managers, regional managers, area managers, and client officers, as well as the accounts manager, Information Technology officer, research analyst, product development officer, and training facilitator. These individuals include: Memg Chanthol, Noun Channy, Meas Chanra, Try Dana, Peang In, Sok Khana, Hun Kolap, Chea Leng, Rann Loca, Choun Sam Onn, Kinsam Onn, Tep Phalla, Yiv Phanna, Vong Pheakyny, Kim Phearum, Chheang Ponharith, Som Praseur, Sok Ratana, Touch Sakhorn, Chiv Samrith, Kang Sang, Yann Sarath, Lim Seaksrun, Thin Seam, Im Seila, Phem Sidorn, Ny Sokea, Rith Sokha, Sin Sokheang, Sou Sokhoeun, Hing Sokutheara, Hin Sokuntheara, Heak Thavuth, Muta Touch, Mith Tuch, Sy Vanthy, Om Vichvy, Roeung Viriny, Khoun Vorn, Chheang Vuthy,

Clients interviewed in three branches. We held focus group discussions and individual interviews with a range of clients (and former clients), including those with leadership positions in village banks, village bank presidents, group loan clients, individual loan clients, savers, and those who had used AMK's transfer services. Again, our focus was on clients who had been with AMK for some time and could give some perspective on how things have changed (or stayed the same) over time; indeed, a number of interviewees were members of the Concern credit and savings programme that transformed into AMK in 2003. We would like to thank the following clients for their valuable insights and for taking the time to recall distant memories of their experiences with AMK. Kandal Branch: Dueh Sithuor, Bun Maeh, Nhean Hin, Tol KimRan, Khiev Him, Nath Lin, Chim Chin, Say Mao, Ke Sokun, Han Vy, Chin Mot, Sen Chanthy, Ya Yap, Uth Sreypov. Kg Speu Branch: Chhay Kosal, Pong Ret, Chhim Mitt, Sou Sarom, Khoung Layhoun. Pursat Branch: Kang Phang, Song Kiev.

Other colleagues and friends. In writing this book we have connected to a broad range of talented individuals within the microfinance industry, and from a wider set of organizations and backgrounds, to help us step outside our own frame of reference, so that we might consider this book from the reader's perspective: what they might be looking for; what might inspire them to start reading AMK's story; and what would keep them reading as this story unfolds. We are particularly grateful for the input of the following people: Caroline Ashely; Deborah Burand; Susan Davis; Anne Hastings; Peter Harlock; David Johnson; Perpetua Kirby; Kate McKee; Jan Piercy; Carl Prechezer; and Tris Lumley. Last but never least: for support logistical, conceptual and otherwise, special thanks are due to Tammy Cameron, Tony Sheldon, Kathryn O'Neill, and Rick Foot (for the tower).

Key people in the history of AMK

Chief Executive Officers
Tanmay Chetan (July 2003–June 2007)
Paul Luchtenburg (July 2007–August 2010)
Pete Power (September 2010–July 2012)
Kea Borann (July 2012–present)

Chairs of the Board
Theresa McDonnell Friström (2003–2004)
Tom O'Higgins (2005–2010)
Tanmay Chetan (2010–present)

Other
Olga Torres (Head of Training, Research and Marketing, 2003–2009,
　　Member Social Performance Committee, 2010–present)
Gerhard Bruckermann (Director, 2004–2010)
Howard Dalzell (Director, 2005–present)
Pete Power (Director, 2006–present)
Adrian Graham (Director, 2006–present)

Prologue: Seila's story

Today is the day we feed the ghosts. The monks have been chanting in the temple all night, and by afternoon we'll meet seven generations of our ancestors as they emerge from the other side. We'll offer to them prayers and food to ease their suffering, before they disappear again. There are far too many ghosts now, too many gone from our families and villages since my mother's time. Even those that remain today are somehow half-ghost – a foot or a leg taken – no longer complete humans.

It is two hours before dawn, and Seila stands vigilant over the fire, tending the rice she is preparing for Pchum Ben – the festival of the ancestors. Her children sleep on inside their bamboo and thatch hut, unaware of the light breeze prising its welcome fingers through the walls. She adjusts the pot on the fire and considers the day ahead. Before making the long walk to the temple, she'll need to go to market. If she can sell enough steamed coconut rice sweets before the festival, she might be able to come home with some fish for the children. She'll send her daughter to the river to fetch the water; there's no school for her to attend anyway. Not since the war.

The year is 2002. Nine years have passed since the UN left Cambodia, and the fragile peace is at least some consolation for the hardship that Seila and so many others face. Lots of things have changed for the better – landmines are less common now – but clean water, quality roads, functioning markets, and good healthcare are still beyond reach for most people living in rural areas.

Seila places the steaming pot on a straw mat beside the fire, and covers it with a board. When it is cool, she will start forming the rice into small balls: some to throw into the air for the spirits; some to feed the monks; and the rest for the community. The secret to making the balls sticky enough to hold their shape is to not stir the rice in the pot as it cooks. She knows this. She had always been proud of her rice.

This should have been my rice, the rice I grew with my own hands. Instead, I traded my last laying hen at market for a bag from the next village. Not the biggest bag, but there should be enough left over to feed the children for a few days. A year ago my life was very hard. Today it is almost impossible. This is not what I had expected on that day when the strangers came to the village. I was surprised when that car rolled into our village last year – I wondered how long it took them to travel from the town. I've heard that it takes half a day or more – and that's when the road is clear. You can never count on that.

When they came, we gathered under the tree outside the village chief's fine wooden house, with its tiled roof and different rooms. The strangers talked to us about money – how they would give us loans for our businesses, so we could earn

http://dx.doi.org/10.3362/ 9781780448640.001

more to buy the things we needed for our families. They were interested in our lives, and they wanted to help us. If we formed small groups, these people would give us each a loan for a year, and when we had used it to make more money we would pay it back, plus a little more. We didn't need to give a physical security for the loan; instead we would be responsible for each other, and the group would work together to make sure we all repaid. I wanted to use my loan to buy fertilizer to improve my paddy field. Rice responds well to hard work: the more you feed it, the more you weed and control the water level – the better your harvest. I was excited that this would finally make my family's life better.

I visited my neighbours and convinced them to join a group with me. We had known each other since we were little girls, and I trusted they were hard-working and honest enough to repay on time (I couldn't say that about all the women in the village!). The people in the car, they visited each house and asked questions about our lives – how much land we have to farm, how many children we have, how often we eat. I think my neighbour Chhean failed the test: they said she wasn't poor enough to join my group. I found another woman instead; although I didn't know her as well, I had seen her at market and remembered that she made delicious fish soup.

It wasn't as easy to get a loan as they said it would be. First we had to set aside our spare savings in a special box at the chief's house. It seemed peculiar, but the idea was that when we had saved enough, we could get a loan. I was worried that I couldn't do this: the floods the year before had been bad – my rice crop failed, and I had to rely on my hens and sewing work to get by. When there was no money at all, I traded my gold necklaces for food. Once I even almost sold my sewing needles. I didn't understand how they could ask me to save, when every day I struggle to feed my children. But the promise of a loan gave me more hope than I'd had since my husband died. I decided to set aside what I could, when I had a little more, and also to dig up the money buried under the house for emergencies. It took time, but I was finally able to set aside enough to get a loan.

The day came – I remember the smell of the jasmine outside the chief's house in the hot sun. The car arrived, dusty from the long journey; the staff emerged with solemn faces, and solemn news. There would be no money that day. Something about the organization not having enough to share with us. We must wait. I was anxious; if I didn't buy fertilizer soon, it would be too late in the planting cycle to use it. Another month passed, and still no money. Perhaps I could have bought a little fertilizer with my savings, but these were locked up in a box in the chief's house. A third month passed, and finally the loans came. Should I take it? The chance to use it for my farming had passed, but I reasoned I would buy more hens, and maybe a hand-powered sewing machine to do more mending work. Those things wouldn't bring in much money, but enough to get by when the crop failed, as it so often did. More importantly, if I didn't take the loan, I was afraid that I would have to leave my group and this chance would pass me by. So I took the loan.

Perhaps it all would have worked out fine. Perhaps I could have used the money to do more trading as I had planned. But my son soon fell ill with fever, and I had to use the money to buy medicine and special food for him. We weren't supposed to use the loan for such things, so when they came by to check on my business I made sure my son was out of sight. With a poor harvest, and no extra money to help my work, I couldn't repay my loan. Worse, being part of the group meant that I had to keep saving every month as well. Where was all this money supposed to come from? And how was it supposed to make my life better to have less money than I did before? At least my son got better, and the fever never spread to my other children.

Finally, I felt I had no other choice. I sold most of my hens (except my best one) to repay the loan. I thought I could use my savings at the chief's house to get by until it was time for the next loan. I thought that as long as it came on time (surely it would, this time?) I could buy fertilizer and my harvest would be better this year. But when I went to the chief's house to collect my savings, I found that they could offer me sweet tea, but not my savings. My money was gone. Without telling us, the chief had lent everyone's savings to his brother-in-law, so he could add to his already considerable herd of cattle. I complained to the client officer, but he said he couldn't help me. He said we need to look after our own savings, and our village committee got to decide how to use them. I was confused. But more than that, I was scared. And so it was a few days ago that I made another decision: I sold my last hen. Rice for the children, rice for the festival. Hopefully things will be better soon. If not, I don't know what I'll do.

∞

Seila's story is not the archetypal 'client success' narrative that development organizations feature on their websites and annual reports – the kind that show the smiling faces of poor people whose lives have been changed for the better by the organization in question. Neither is it untrue. This particular story involves a so-called 'beneficiary' of the Concern Worldwide microcredit programme, which operated in Cambodia between 1993 and 2003 (and which was the pre-cursor to AMK, the organization at the heart of this book). More worryingly, Seila's experience is not uncommon. Her tale features a number of stock elements we can easily identify: poor people living in desperate conditions, a charity programme committed to improving their lives, and a negative result that no one had anticipated.

So what went wrong? How did this charity programme, with the best intentions in the world, fail to stand by those good intentions; fail to deliver the loan at the time it was so urgently needed; fail to protect Seila from fraud by her fellow villagers? And why is this such a common story? How is it that so many organizations, seeking to do good in the world, often miss opportunities to do so — and in fact exacerbate the very problem they seek to address?

This is the fundamental question that drove us to write this book – and we recognize that coming to grips with the answer is of increasing importance.

Countless organizations of every shape, size and orientation are in the business of going good – working with poor and vulnerable communities around the world, delivering potentially life-changing services to address a range of pressing social needs. Some are doing excellent work, and this book examines what it is that they do that makes the difference.

But at the same time, a common theme has emerged in our work over the past 20 years: we see organizations missing opportunities to do things better and organizations getting things wrong, again and again. Seila's story is one of many we have come across, and no doubt countless remain untold elsewhere. Stories about poor families using their charity-distributed, insecticide-treated bed net to dry fish in the sun. Stories of Dalits (so-called untouchables) shut out from community development projects when village leaders don't even think to mention that they exist. Stories of microfinance providers that over-indebt their clients and then strip them of the few assets they have when they fail to repay their loans. And we're not talking about the unscrupulous private moneylenders charging exorbitant interest rates to the poorest of the poor – we're talking about the organizations that are actually trying to *help* people. Shouldn't we be doing better than *not quite good enough?*

When we survey the landscape of missed opportunities, it might be tempting to simply accept these types of stories as the inevitable result of organizations trying their best: 'sometimes they get it wrong, and there's nothing to be done about that'. However, when organizations enter the lives of poor and vulnerable people, there is a moral and ethical imperative to make good on good intentions, and not to make people's lives worse as a result. Recognizing this is perhaps easier than admitting that despite those good intentions, we as organizations have too often failed to create lasting and positive change in the world. It was hearing the experiences of Seila (and women and men just like her), that led Concern Worldwide to turn shortcomings into a success story, through its vision and support for AMK. For other organizations to make the same journey, we need to learn the lessons from those who are doing good well. In this book, we will explore why the detail of how we work makes a difference, and how small changes can make a big impact on people's lives. If the time is right for organizations to step back, reflect, and learn from one other about how to achieve better outcomes for the people we serve, then here is one such story.

Introduction: Going beyond good intentions

Seila's story highlights a surprising problem: when it comes to making the world a better place good intentions are not enough. This is our point of departure for this book. Framing our narrative are the pressing social needs of large swathes of the world's population: secure livelihoods, healthy food, stable health, clean water, adequate knowledge, political voice, and social equality – all the basic elements that support human existence. This is a story about organizations that strive to create a positive impact on the people they serve and the wider world around them – the organizations that tackle the failures of the market (and the public sector) which overlook the needs of poor and excluded people. Their vision is clear: engage with vulnerable communities, and deliver vital services in order to improve different aspects of their lives.

However, we know from experience that many organizations are falling short of their promises. Some fail to deliver the social value they aspire to, others find their potential impact curtailed by reaching only small pockets of individuals. More worryingly, some risk making those they serve worse off as a result of their initiatives: through products that are ill-adapted to clients' needs, delivered in a manner that is culturally or economically inadequate, or unsustainable to the point that they fail to be anything more than 'flash-in-the-pan' interventions. Where this happens, it's not just the people we serve that suffer – so too does the entire industry we have created to help them, as public confidence in our work ebbs away. The question before us then, is clear: how can social purpose organizations do more good, and less harm?

Before tackling this question, however, another one seems more pressing: who should care? This book is based on the experience of a particular type of organization: so-called social enterprises that seek to use the power of the market to deliver social good. But it is also a call to action for a broader set of organizations, because we recognize that the institutional landscape is changing as the lines between different business models become blurred. There is increasing awareness that our future – as individuals, communities, companies, countries, and indeed as a planet – is shaped by the complex interactions through which we as individuals live, work and produce. Everything is intertwined: we cannot separate commercial businesses from the human landscape in which we operate, nor the economic lives of individuals from their personal lives. In this way, 'doing good' in the world is no longer the sole preserve of so-called 'do-gooder' organizations. Even for-profit companies have a vested interest in doing good in the world, because building a market for their products isn't viable in the long term if those products destroy the lives of the people within it, or the environment and community surrounding it. Conversely, enhancing the livelihoods of clients and their communities strengthens the ecosystem within which a business operates. In this way, we see increasing traction around the idea that doing good, and avoiding harm, is a natural foundation for a long-term and sustainable commercial strategy. A failure to recognize this not only exposes clients to potentially negative outcomes, but represents a lost opportunity to create synergies between strategies that are good for both people and profit.

So too blurred is the nomenclature employed by various sectors to describe the final goal of 'doing good': some call it 'social change'; some, 'impact'; others, 'value creation'. Within these pages, we will refrain from presenting conceptually elegant definitions of these terms. Fundamentally, it's not about what an organization calls itself, what its profit motive is, or how it describes its *raison d'être* to its stakeholders. This book is relevant to any organisation interested in sustainably maximising people's well-being through the mechanism of the marketplace.

The common thread is this: any organization (of whatever type) seeking to harness the opportunity and dynamism of business to create social value, seeks ways to do so more effectively. There is already a lot of dialogue in different sectors tackling different aspects of this question; this book aims to add insights around what it takes to build an organization that will do good, and do well, within the marketplace. Our radical proposition is this: that putting a 'social value lens' on business requires more than simply delivering beneficial products and services to people that need them. It means designing an organization whose entire business model is aligned with the overriding social value narrative. Once the frame of focus shifts from 'good products' to 'good organizations', the landscape changes. New challenges arise when we apply a social value lens to the strategic and operational questions that organizations ask when designing a business model because, in doing so, we will come up with remarkably different answers.

To explore what using this new social value lens means in practice, this book will look at one organization, in one country, in one industry: Angkor Mikroheranhvatho Kampuchea (AMK), a microfinance organization in Cambodia.

Microfinance has an explicit social mission to reduce the poverty and vulnerability of its clients. Different microfinance organizations target different types of clients (some poor, some less poor). Some offer only financial products (loans, savings, money transfers, insurance); others add non-financial services (e.g. business, literacy or health training) to the mix. Either way, the overall aim is to give clients access to the tools and skills they need to cope with the unexpected, better manage their finances, and invest in opportunities to increase their income. As a pioneering sector in building financially sustainable (and profitable) organizations that leverage commercial capital to reach and benefit hundreds of millions of people around the world, microfinance offers key lessons around both doing good and doing well in the marketplace. Moreover, as a sector that is explicitly in the business of putting poor and vulnerable people into debt, microfinance can throw up sharp and useful insights on how to avoid doing harm.

The Cambodian microfinance sector provides an interesting case study precisely because it lays bare the tension between profit, value and harm. It is a mature and highly crowded marketplace, with some 42 institutions competing in a country of 15 million people. In a market where only the strong will flourish, any microfinance organization seeking to deliver social value cannot but grapple with the reality of balancing profit and impact.

AMK was launched in the heyday of international microfinance expansion and commercialization; however, it recognized the weaknesses of the typical approach, which viewed social value creation as a more or less automatic process. AMK's story is worth telling because, as an organization, it tested a radical notion: that doing what was good for its clients would be good for business. It went beyond good intentions, taking a deliberate approach to reach poor people and deliver on its promise of improving their lives. More often than not, this focus has driven the organization to take decisions around its business model that were out of line with those taken by its competitors, or that even defied internationally agreed best practice for microfinance. In doing so, AMK became the largest microfinance organization in the country (in terms of number of clients reached), while at the same time achieving deep outreach to poor people and generating profit as a business. This is not to say that it always got things right, but AMK has learned from its experiences and missteps, and has come out stronger and more effective. For these reasons, we believe that this organization, in this market, in this sector, provides solid insights into what it means to build a business model for good.

Building a business model for good

So when we talk about building a business model that works 'for good', what exactly do we mean? Firstly, as with any commercial business, products and services are important. But as social enterprises, we need to push the boundaries in terms of how we conceptualize and deliver our products, and make product design work from the perspective of *who* we are working with, *what* their needs are, and *how* we can design our services in a way that promotes good and avoids harm. It's also about whether we can reach our target market, and effectively address barriers to access – whether these be cultural, economic, geographical, or gender-related. More concretely, we need to help clients access the *value potential* of our products and services. In part this is about ensuring that clients use our products as intended; but it also means ensuring that they are *delivered* as intended, and that we manage the quality of delivery. It's also about making peace with the fact that, as an organization, we're not always going to get it right the first time; recognizing and correcting mistakes is all part of the process. For this reason, space for reflection and innovation should be built into the business model.

Building a business model to deliver good also means engaging with communities over the long run, especially where we seek to promote long-term changes. For this to happen, we need to ensure that the financial model makes sense, that we can cover the costs of serving our clients, and harness economies of scale. We also need to recognize that profit can be a tool to help achieve social value, and that we can strike the right balance between our social goals and profitability. Finally, being an effective social purpose organization involves understanding that, however noble and important our mission might be, the world does *not* revolve around us. Regulators, policy-makers, competitors, the media, the general public, and even our clients, will help or hinder the work we are trying to accomplish. The landscape that surrounds us will be in constant motion, and we need to respond appropriately to external influences in a way which preserves our core identity as social purpose organizations – even if this means *completely* changing what we are doing in response to failure or promising new opportunities.

AMK highlights the importance of not putting your social value pro-position in a silo, but using it to drive every aspect of your organization's strategy and operations. By doing this, and doing it well, AMK found that it was not only delivering more valuable products and services (to the right people and in the right way), but also that it could rationalize the internal contradictions and tensions that might undermine and distort the 'goodness' enshrined in its products, and which might, ultimately, produce outcomes other than those expected.

This, in brief, is the social value lens we can apply to our business models to help us do good better, and avoid doing harm. The chapters that follow will explore these ideas in more depth, and present six key insights aimed at helping organizations understand what putting this new lens into practice looks like. These insights are summarized briefly below.

Insight 1: Don't just offer products; respond to client needs

As service providers, it is all too easy to lead with those services; simply to supply what we as organizations believe to be the best response to a given problem, or to fall prey to an easy 'off-the-shelf' product. Commercial businesses thrive by selling products that customers want and are sufficiently satisfied with to buy again. As organizations seeking to create social value, however, we need to go beyond what clients *want* or *like*. Rather we should ask: what do they actually *need* in order to face the unique vulnerabilities present in their lives? What do they need in order to grasp the opportunities in front of them? To a large extent, this means shedding our assumptions about our clients: starting with their needs (expressed and unexpressed), and working backwards from there to develop our product solutions.

As a financial service provider, AMK invested in generating a detailed picture of its clients' financial lives: not just how they earned income, but what those income streams looked like over the course of the year in terms of typical windfalls and crunch points. This research actually turned a lot of common stereotypes of about rural Cambodians neatly upside down – namely by highlighting that clients had mixed economic baskets rather than relying purely on agricultural income. By understanding the opportunities and constraints faced by clients in their financial lives, AMK was able identify weaknesses in its offering and create a product line that was targeted, flexible and, more importantly, distinct; a product line that not only worked for clients, but gave AMK a crucial competitive advantage within the marketplace.

Insight 2: Ask good questions; have good conversations

In terms of smart product and service design, getting to grips with the realities of clients' lives is an essential first step, but it's not the whole picture. As social purpose organizations, we need to keep in mind certain key questions: 'what is working?' and 'what is working for whom?' Not only this, but we need to use these insights to make better decisions about how to adjust our products and services as we develop. This requires a fundamental shift in ongoing conversations around what 'good organizational performance' means, and putting in place the structures to ensure this happens.

AMK took a deliberate approach to ensuring that the understanding about clients generated by its research fed into product design and adjustment. A key innovation here was the creation of a special committee at Board level, which served to institutionalize this conversation. Its function is to shape the direction of AMK's research, ensure its quality, and then help 'translate' the results for the rest of the Board. As AMK's research questions have moved from trying to understand clients towards trying to understand what is happening in their lives as a result of its work, there has been a greater need for interconnectivity between its Research and Operations departments, and the committee acts as an effective bridge in this respect.

Insight 3: Do what it says on the tin

Why is it that the best laid plans go awry? Too often we see a disjunction between what an organization *says* it does (offering products that look great on paper), and what *actually happens* in practice (when those products are put into the hands of staff). Thoughtfully-designed products and services are of course essential – but when it comes to ensuring positive outcomes for clients, the devil is in the detail about *how* they are delivered, and whether the value proposition is being lost by a lack of understanding on the ground. Sometimes too, good intentions become distorted by our own operational infrastructure, particularly when we're training staff do one thing, but pushing them to do the opposite (through misaligned incentives, for example). Quality delivery is not automatic, especially when what we're asking our staff to do is difficult.

AMK's business model calls for its field staff to do physically and intellectually demanding work: travelling long distances over difficult terrain, working efficiently and respectfully with large numbers of clients, and solving problems as they arise. AMK learned from its mistakes that key elements of delivery needed to be managed. For example, responding to the challenge of staff cutting corners in the name of efficiency, AMK established incentive and monitoring systems focusing on *how* the job is done, not just whether targets are met. Another example relates to good loan appraisals, which are meant to strike the right balance between providing clients with enough credit and not imposing too much debt. To get this balance right, AMK needed to know that staff weren't just doing the appraisals as a box-ticking exercise, but were doing them well, in such a way as to avoid over-indebting clients.

Insight 4: Motivate staff to do difficult work in an excellent way

When it comes to ensuring that staff are equipped to manage the tension between our commercial and social objectives, it's not just the so-called 'hard systems' (such as incentives) that count. In the context of difficult work, there's only so far that we can automate quality, and we need staff who can critically reflect on their work when 'reality gaps' arise between theory and practice. Hard systems can shape staff understanding of *what* they need to do – but we also need staff who understand *why* it is important, and who engage in an organization-wide dialogue around how to do their work better. We don't always get the model right the first time, and listening to ideas around innovation from the frontlines is particularly important because design flaws and inconsistencies will be clearest to those working directly with our clients. This means having the right people with the right outlook, and fostering an organizational culture that supports, rather than undermines, our social value proposition.

AMK put effort into building a culture that would support its people to do excellent work. It started by challenging the rigid hierarchy common to many Cambodian organizations by instilling instead a 'family' feel, where staff are valued equally. Regardless of their position, all staff wear the same informal company shirt, making it impossible to pick out the 'boss of the office'. They also refer to each other not with honorific titles denoting rank, but as 'brother' and 'sister'. Not only do staff feel equal, and equally valued, they are also encouraged to reflect critically on their work and share their ideas about how to do it better – knowing that within the meritocracy of AMK, the best idea wins. To support this, AMK has created an infrastructure to gather staff feedback: through 'open house' events, staff satisfaction surveys, feedback boxes, and a 'whistle-blowing' policy that allows staff to raise serious concerns. It also trains senior staff on how to give and receive feedback, to ensure that there are no bottlenecks in the lines of communication between different levels of the organization.

Insight 5: Own the dirt road

When it comes to tackling pressing and widespread social problems, great optimism can often be clouded by voices of doubt whispering in our collective ear: *'It just can't be done. You'll never make it sustainable.'* These are the 'dirt roads' that we are told are too difficult to travel along. But the whole point about a social enterprise is to reject 'business as usual' and find a way to make business work for those who are marginalized. Our challenge, then, is to start with the goal and work backwards from there: to design a business model that really works in challenging environments. This means thinking through questions around where to grow, how to grow, and what trade-offs to accept in terms of efficiency and quality – all from the perspective of delivering social value. It also means striking the right balance between simple and complex services, and thinking through what we mean by 'going for scale': is it meeting many needs of a few people, or a few needs of many people? The message here is find your own dirt road – the one you're told you can't possibly navigate – and make the journey work for what you want to achieve.

For AMK, the 'unreachable frontier' was to serve poor rural people in a commercially viable manner. Conventional wisdom was that it just couldn't be done. Poor people wanted small loans, and it was just too costly to deliver those in remote areas in a sustainable way. AMK recognized that the costs were high, but nevertheless created a business model that worked. It countered small profit margins with scale of outreach and efficiency. It countered the increased risk of lending to poor people with services that worked in areas of low competition, thereby garnering real client loyalty. It also reduced its risks as a lender by reducing clients' risks by offering services that were designed to help clients succeed, even when they hit bumps in the road.

Insight 6: Adapt to the changing landscape

Just because we have a full picture of what challenges clients face, and what services they need, doesn't necessarily mean that we'll be able to meet *all* of those needs at a given time. What we decide to do today (and in five years' time) depends on a number of internal and external variables that are constantly in motion. In some instances, we'll recognize not only a client need, but also the limits of what our organization is best placed to deliver in the context of the many needs that clients face. Down the line, we may re-think what we do in light of evolution in our organizational capacity, technology, client capacity or external factors such as regulation and competition.

Over the course of its history, AMK has evolved from a largely credit-only provider to one offering a broad range of financial services through a number of delivery channels. Its understanding of its clients' needs has remained unchanged, but as its organizational capacity has grown and regulatory barriers have dropped (for instance around the provision of savings, mobile banking services and microinsurance), AMK has piloted and added new products to its offering to respond in a more holistic way to its clients' varied financial needs.

So does it work?

In light of our fundamental question around how social enterprises can do more good (and less harm), what's most interesting about AMK's 'great experiment' is not that it chose to run it, but that (by a number of measures), it does actually seem to be working. Its success can be seen in three dimensions: reaching the people that it seeks to serve, creating a sustainable business, and supporting positive changes in the lives of its clients.

Outreach to poor people

Today AMK provides loans, savings and transfer services to more than 370,000 households. In a country with a population of 15 million, this means it serves around 10 per cent of all households. Moreover, AMK's network of 128 branches and sub-branches allows it to serve an impressive 80 per cent of Cambodian villages.

Since 2007, the strapline 'Finance at your doorstep' has featured on the front cover of AMK's annual reports. This is far from being a hollow marketing gimmick. Overcoming barriers to access for rural poor people meant taking financial services deep into rural areas, rather than setting up branches in easier-to-reach towns and rural market centres and waiting for clients to come to AMK. Today, even after expanding to cover most of the country, over 90 per cent of AMK's borrowers reside in rural areas. But AMK didn't just go rural, it went big. What is particularly interesting is the *type* of growth it sought to achieve – scale in terms of numbers of clients, rather than portfolio size. In line with this strategy, in 2009 AMK became the microfinance organization with the largest client outreach in the country, while still only ranking fifth in portfolio size. That is, it sought to reach out to more poor people rather than to serve 'upmarket' clients who wanted bigger loans.

But it's not only that AMK sought to reach more clients, and more rural clients. It also sought to reach *poorer* clients. By going into areas where poverty incidence was highest, and through smart product design that encourages poor clients to self-select into its programme (as we'll explore in Chapter 1), AMK's poverty outreach has always trended above national averages. In 2007, the average Cambodian had a 50 per cent chance of being poor. In the same year, the average new AMK client had a 75 per chance of being poor. Impressively, AMK actually *increased* its depth of outreach to poor people in its middle years, even as national poverty levels began to fall. Today, nearly half of all AMK's new group loan clients are below the rural food poverty line.

Profitability

To grow to scale and provide millions of dollars of loans, AMK must access capital from investors who have high benchmarks on financial risk and return. Its objective to reach rural poor people was costly, and could only be achieved through a strong focus on efficiency and productivity. Given its challenging business model, it is remarkable that AMK has achieved levels of financial return considered respectable by international standards in microfinance. In 2013, AMK achieved a profit in excess of US$3.3 million, and a return on equity of 18 per cent. The commercial success of AMK is evident in the interest shown by a number of investors (both social and commercial) who see the business potential of its approach.

What's interesting here is not just that AMK is profitable, but that it has clearly defined its relationship with profitability from a social value perspective. As a social enterprise, financial return is the means to deliver on its social mission rather than a goal in itself. AMK needs to achieve a level of return that allows for expansion and development, secures investment, and guarantees the financial stability of the company. Beyond this, profit is viewed as an opportunity to create more social value for clients. As such, the Board generally expects to see a 15–20 per cent return on equity, beyond which it passes on excessive returns (if they arise) to clients in the form of improved products or price reductions.

Benefits for clients

Of course, if AMK's services were not actually benefiting its clients in line with its mission, then the fact that the organization had reached scale, found an efficient and profitable business model, and successfully reached its target market would be a hollow achievement. Not only did AMK invest in understanding its clients at the start, but it undertook detailed research to track changes in the lives of a sample of clients over time. An AMK study (completed in 2012 and published in 2014) looked at changes over a six-year period, and provides useful insights as to how clients might be benefiting.

Considering contextual changes

AMK is careful not to make grand claims of impact, particularly given the complexity of unpicking the causes of changes in the lives of clients with different profiles and experiences. It's also important to consider how the broader context of national economic growth comes into play. The AMK research covered a time during which Cambodia's economy registered strong positive growth; between 2004 and 2011, the number of people living in poverty more than halved.[1] This was evidenced in the survey results, which painted a picture of a rural population with increased spending power, and who were building assets and educating their children. During this time, annual expenditure increased across the board, particularly on food, clothing and footwear. As promising as that sounds, most families had actually been lifted out of poverty by only a small margin, and instead of being 'poor' were now considered 'near-poor'. Their lives were still vulnerable, with a real risk of falling back into poverty at the slightest income shock. To put this into context: an average loss of just $0.30 in daily income would tip 3 million near-poor Cambodians back into poverty, doubling the country's 2013 poverty rate from 20.5% to about 40%.[2]

Against a backdrop of overall positive changes in Cambodia (see Box 'Considering contextual changes') AMK's study highlights areas where clients have experienced greater positive change than non-clients. Firstly, clients are now more able to invest in their future. Take the example of investing in children's education: 57 per cent of respondents in 2012 expect all their children to complete secondary education, compared to 17 per cent in 2006. This is a sizeable jump from the baseline, even though a considerable (albeit lower) improvement can also be seen in the non-client group (up to 40 per cent from 31 per cent).

Increased ability to afford large expenses (e.g. a new house, land, or a tractor) points towards the same theme: that clients now have greater stability and control over their finances. Among clients this increase is remarkable, from 4 per cent at the beginning of the study period to 24 per cent at the end. Against this 20 per cent increase, there was an increase of only 11 per cent in the non-client group. Overall, the study findings indicate that AMK clients enjoy greater participation in the market economy, and also the ability to undertake long-term investments in health, transport and communication, which should continue to yield further livelihood dividends in the future.

These economic gains are reflected in a significant change in client well-being.[3] Among clients, 74 per cent reported improvements (and 26 per cent a decline); whereas among non-clients, only 41 per cent experienced an improvement (and 59 per cent a decline). Clients are also now spending more on food compared to non-clients. We also see a small (but significant) positive change in the poverty status of AMK clients: numbers in the 'very poor' category declined from 41 to 37 per cent, and in the 'poor' category from 37 to 32 per cent, whereas numbers in the 'less poor' category actually increased from 22 to 31 per cent. In comparison, there is no recorded change in poverty status over time for non-clients.[4] Moreover, AMK's data on poverty shows that the poorest clients are making faster gains than other client groups, and more so than the poorest non-clients. These results are all the more interesting when we consider that a third of the non-client sample group are actually clients of other microfinance organizations, so there's an extent to which these results should be interpreted not just as exploring 'does AMK have a positive influence on the lives of the poor?', but also 'does AMK have a positive influence compared to that of other providers?'

Despite income and consumption improvements, survey results also show that challenges remain. In particular, the data points to increased levels of vulnerability to external shocks, in that people are more often affected by climate events (both flooding and drought) and household health events. AMK's study looked at whether the household had faced a crisis or major event in the previous year. The data shows that frequency of emergencies approximately doubled across both client and non-client groups. Borrowing and sale of assets to cover health costs also increased in both groups.

A brief history

Chapters 1 to 6 explore key insights around how to create effective social enterprises, using AMK's experience as a point of departure. These insights will help organizations put the right lens on their strategy and operations, ask the right questions, and to find answers that make sense for them as organizations and for their clients. In an effort to contextualize these themes, we thought it important to provide a brief chronological account of AMK's development – touching upon key milestones in the evolution of its business model that contribute to our six key insights, as well as the enabling factors that surrounded and supported this development (see Table 'Milestones in AMK's history').

As a microfinance organization and a social enterprise, AMK has reached scale in a dynamic and competitive market after several cycles of innovation over the course of which its business model has changed considerably. The path it travelled to reach this stage was not linear: it was signposted by the typical 'zig-zags' of an evolving organization that sets and changes its strategy; responds to changing internal capacity and the external environment; and both makes, and learns from, its mistakes. This journey can be framed within four broad phases: laying the foundations, growing to become Cambodia's largest microfinance organisation, stress-testing the model, and diversification and growth in a competitive market.

Laying the foundations

Our narrative begins in the decade leading up to the 2003 formation of AMK, which saw a credit and savings programme run by the charity Concern Worldwide transform into a registered microfinance organization. This transition was notable for the way in which the parent organization developed a supportive framework enabling the creation of an autonomous subsidiary that was able to remain focused on its founding mission and values, while at the same time establishing a commercial business (see Box 'AMK-Concern Framework Agreement, 2003').

AMK's genesis came 13 years after a UN peace accord closed the door on a decade of political violence and economic deprivation that had left millions of Cambodians dead, and thousands more at the mercy of the landmines punctuating the landscape. While the decade following the first elections in 1993 saw real progress in terms of resettling displaced populations, restoring basic economic infrastructure, and nurturing the fragile political system (which while offering relative stability, was still marred by factional violence), real challenges remained. More than a third of the population were unable to secure enough food for even basic subsistence (and a much higher proportion lived below the international $1 per day poverty line).[5]

The benefits of moderate economic growth had, by and large, failed to extend beyond urban centres; over 90 per cent of poor people lived in rural areas.

AMK's development was influenced by the timing of its entrance into the marketplace, just before an explosion of growth in the national microfinance sector (mirroring that of the international sector). When AMK was registered in 2003, the microfinance market was relatively undeveloped, and most microfinance organizations had achieved neither significant scale nor financial sustainability. As AMK inherited a reasonably large and active client base from Concern Cambodia, it had the benefit of starting at a stage which would otherwise have taken years to build up: 65 staff, 10,000 clients and a loan portfolio of around $670,000. However, the quality of the portfolio was poor and the systems weak, so AMK had to build a lot of systems and processes from the ground up. As it did so, it benefited from the opportunity to learn from the experience (and mistakes) of other organizations, as there was already a large and well-documented body of so-called 'best practice' available in the public domain.

AMK's early years were marked by a focus on developing two core elements of its business model. Firstly, it was determined to shape its products and services on the basis of a deep understanding of the lives and needs of poor, rural Cambodians; it was keen not to make assumptions about its clients, or assume that other organizations had already found the best answers. Secondly, it focused on building efficient systems, so that it could not only deliver quality services to its clients, but scale its outreach to deliver services to *more* clients.

AMK-Concern Framework Agreement, 2003

In recognition of the difference between running a charity project and a permanent organization functioning as a business, the relationship between Concern and AMK (as a wholly owned subsidiary) was carefully designed and managed from the outset. Three core risks were identified, and addressed through a Framework Agreement which codified this relationship.

Firstly, the agreement acknowledged that AMK was an independent organization in its own right; it was no longer a programme to be managed by Concern. AMK had freedom to define its own internal policies, procedures, and strategy and was to be treated as a subsidiary company with accountability to its own Board, rather than a local Country Director.

Secondly, it recognized that it would be difficult for AMK to raise commercial or donor capital from outside. For that reason, Concern committed funding to cover loan capital and operating losses for the first three years, after which AMK would be expected to be financially sustainable in terms of its operations, and to seek international investment to support an envisaged period of rapid growth.

Thirdly, the agreement placed emphasis on AMK's mission, which was focused on delivering financial services to improve the livelihood options of poor people, and building a financially sustainable institution that would achieve scale and be a major player in the market place.

These years of foundation-building were facilitated by financial support provided by Concern, which fully covered both the operating losses and capital requirements for a rapidly growing organization. Having this financial security gave Management the critical space to focus on getting the business right – the value of which cannot be overstated.

In terms of results, this phase was marked by successful product innovation in AMK's core group lending methodology, and the development of its 'credit line' product in 2005, offering individual flexibility for clients that was (and is to this day) seldom seen in microfinance. At the same time, AMK achieved its target of becoming financially self-sufficient 18 months after registration, and built the necessary systems to allow for a 50 per cent growth in staff and doubling of client numbers between 2003 and 2005. The foundations of a successful new business had been laid.

Growing to become Cambodia's largest microfinance organization

While it is difficult to neatly parcel AMK's development into specific periods, the next phase broadly spans a period of economic boom in Cambodia lasting from 2005 until 2009. During this time, steady and significant growth was mainly driven by outreach to remote areas with low competition, and a commitment to quality. AMK's organizational systems and culture continued to evolve with a focus on research, organizational learning, and institutionalizing conversations around organizational priorities and client experience. For example, a special committee of the Board (the Social Performance Committee, or SPC) was established in late 2005 to help keep AMK on track to meet its social goals.

This period is particularly notable for success in poverty outreach, as AMK's expansion strategy prioritized new branches in the most deprived areas. Growth was also characterized by the establishment of a nationwide branch infrastructure that provided potential for the future. As we shall learn later, this outreach has been fundamental to AMK's success and continues to provide new opportunities.

Strategically, as AMK looked towards its clients and its business model, two decisions clouded its focus and put pressure on its systems. Responding in part to client demand for larger loans (and as part of a risk-reducing portfolio diversification strategy), in 2007 AMK started to make significant expansion in individual lending. However, this product (launched in 2004) turned out to be a weak link. It replicated systems that had proved effective in group lending, rather than developing effective systems for a new model. At the same time, recognizing clients' wider needs (and partly in response to the opportunity of grant funding), AMK began to form partnerships with international organizations to set up stand-alone, non-financial, and bespoke financial projects. While the number of clients involved was small, this was a change in strategy that was not closely interrogated by the Board, and demanded significant Management time.

By 2009, the impact of the global economic crisis was felt, and AMK (alongside its peers) saw a loss of portfolio quality.

Stress testing the model

In the period leading up to the global financial crisis, the organization started to focus on growth as an end in itself, rather than as a product of quality. Financial success bred complacency, and changes in the Board meant a lack of continuity so that issues of concern did not receive the follow-up and attention they needed. It is also possible that Management and the Board were distracted by some of the partnership projects. The culture of research, learning, and dialogue around what works for clients seemed to have faded into the background. Cracks began to develop: management processes overlooked important details such as the quality of loan appraisals; products were launched without careful research and understanding of client need and demand; the new partnerships for non-financial services were not seen within the bigger picture of AMK's business model.

All other things being equal, this erosion of quality might have gone unnoticed. But a perfect storm was brewing: increasing competition and multiple borrowing drove higher levels of client debt for individual clients and, when combined with a loss of client income in the wake of the financial crisis, resulted in an alarming fall in profitability in 2009. This was a turning point, sparking a renewed focus on the core products, core values and core governance and management systems of the organization.

Diversification and growth in a competitive market

The most recent chapter of AMK's short history is one of innovation and evolution in a fast-changing environment. Growth of the microfinance sector and fierce competition means the options for growth are much more challenging: today, 7 of the 15 leading microfinance organizations each cover more than 70 per cent of Cambodia's 24 provinces.

Over time the business model has evolved considerably. The foundation has always been an understanding of AMK's target clients and their needs. But what AMK delivers in response is a factor of internal capacity, technology, and external influences such as regulation and competition. In recent years there has been a transformation of the business as AMK moves to become an organization that provides a full suite of financial services to its clients through multiple channels. This has allowed AMK to work more intensively with its core clients and to deepen value – for both clients and the institution. AMK's growth since 2010 has focused on leveraging its size to diversify its services, rather than focusing on growth in client numbers and portfolio size.

Milestones in AMK's history

1979	Vietnamese army ousts the Khmer Rouge and occupies Cambodia leading to civil war. Vietnamese leave in 1989.
1990	Concern Worldwide opens programme in Cambodia.
1991 – 1993	In 1991, Paris Peace Accord ends the war and sets in place a process leading to democratic elections and UN peacekeeping mission. Democratic elections take place and UN peacekeepers leave Cambodia in 1993.
1997 – 1999	Concern integrates a pilot microcredit scheme into its ongoing community development work in Cambodia, and later separates its microcredit work into an operationally separate savings and credit programme.
2002	New microfinance law requires all non-governmental organization (NGO) microfinance programmes with portfolios in excess of 1 billion riel (then approximately US$254,000) to transform into private companies. Concern registers its programme in December, and has 12 months to complete the transformation process.
2003	AMK is registered as a company fully owned by Concern Worldwide, which occupies all Board seats. AMK inherits 3 branches (provinces), 40 staff, a portfolio of $670,000 and 10,000 clients from Concern (after write-offs, client numbers reduce to 8,848). Tanmay Chetan recruited as (CEO). AMK focuses on financial discipline: e.g. returns seven 4x4 vehicles to Concern. Strategic plan commits to seven-fold increase in clientele by 2008. Funding committed from DEPFA bank to cover operating and capital costs until 2005.
2004	AMK opens in two more provinces (5 branches in total). Gerhard Bruckermann joins Board (first non-Concern member and a banker). Individual credit product launched.
2005	Credit line launched, providing greater flexibility and reducing vulnerability for clients. Social Performance Committee established. Life insurance (death relief fund) product trialled, but stopped due to regulation. Emergency loan and death write-off policies introduced. AMK breaks even. First commercial loan. Tom O'Higgins replaces Theresa McDonnell Friström as Chair of Board.
2006	Government launch year of microcredit, highlighting success of sector and government support. AMK expands to 12 provinces, continues strong growth. Staff productivity levels peak at 937 clients per client officer.
2007	Paul Luchtenburg replaces Tanmay Chetan as CEO. Partnership arrangements to deliver non-financial services. AMK expands branch outreach to 15 provinces, becoming the microfinance organization with greatest geographical coverage in Cambodia.
2008	AMK borrows total of $10 million to support growth. Rapid increase in individual loan exposure and in borrowings. Loan portfolio reaches $23 million.

(Continued)

Milestones in AMK's history (Continued)

2009	AMK becomes largest microfinance organization in Cambodia in terms of client numbers. Impact of 2008 global economic crisis is felt in Cambodia. Portfolio at risk of all microfinance organizations increases; AMK's increases from 0.07% to 2.3%. AMK profit levels fall to worryingly low levels. Individual loan product suspended. Concern decides to sell majority of shares to Agora, a new social investor led by former CEO and funded by former Board member (process delayed until 2012 due to regulatory issues). AMK achieves national coverage, with branch offices in all 24 provinces.
2010	Pete Power steps into the role of CEO. Partnership arrangements for non-financial services terminated. Zero tolerance re-introduced for non-compliance with policy for individual household visit for loan appraisal. AMK receives deposit-taking licence and begins strategic transformation, turning from a rural credit-only business into a broader provider of microfinance. Board approves new 'secondary target' savings clients in order to raise local currency for on-lending and reduce dependence on foreign investors. Tanmay Chetan becomes Chair of Board. Open House process instigated to foster dialogue between branch staff and Management.
2011	New branch-based savings products launched, accompanied by branch building upgrades. AMK's sub-offices converted into front-end offices, increasing its office network from 24 to 98. New mobile banking products introduced. After floods affect 18 of Cambodia's 24 provinces, NGOs publish report *Drowning in Debt* (Di Certo, 2011), raising concerns about over-indebtedness and the response of microfinance organizations. AMK is the only microfinance organization offering low-interest loans to flood-affected families to overcome the effects; generates high customer satisfaction/loyalty. 360-degree appraisal introduced to encourage two-way discussion between staff and line-managers. Core leadership diversified with two new positions and two new hires at the top management level (CEO, Chief Financial Officer, Chief Business Officer, Chief Operating Officer). AMK launches pilot for agent-based savings and money transfer services.
2012	Kea Borann replaces Pete Power as CEO. For the first time, AMK is led by a Cambodian. Executive team management structure introduced, and appointment of Chief Business Officer. Credit Bureau launched in Cambodia.
2013	New investors agreed as Concern finally becomes minority shareholder. AMK introduces ATMs for the first time. Mobile banking through agents is rolled out nationally. AMK releases its first 'Change Study', looking at changes to clients' lives.
2014	AMK becomes a national multi-channel, multi-product financial institution: Agent-based money transfers and agent-based savings roll out nationally after National Bank of Cambodia approval in late 2013. AMK receives microinsurance licence and pilots health and accident insurance.

Notes

1. Based on World Bank data from 2013, [online] <http://data.worldbank.org/country/cambodia> [accessed 1 December 2014]
2. *ibid.*
3. Well-being being measured as a combination of a number of 22 indicators covering expenses, assets, food security, social capital and overall vulnerability (crisis occurrence & coping mechanisms).
4. AMK benchmarks its well-being data against the national poverty line.
5. Sobering reading on national poverty incidence, and other post-war social challenges, is available in the Kingdom of Cambodia National Poverty Reduction Strategy (2003–2007) [online] <www.imf.org/external/np/prsp/2002/khm/01/122002.pdf> [accessed 1 October 2014]

References

AMK (2014) 'AMK Client Change Study 2012' [online publication] <www.amkcambodia.com> [accessed 31 August 2014]

Di Certo, B. (2012) 'Flood-affected poor "drowning in debt"', *Phnom Penh Post* [online] <http://bit.ly/pppost> (23 February 2012) [accessed 1 October 2014]

PART I
Shedding assumptions about clients

For any business to be successful, it first needs to get its products right. From a purely commercial perspective, this statement doesn't seem particularly ground-breaking. In order to generate profit, a business needs to sell things that customers want to buy – and that they'll like enough to buy again. The closer a business can come to understanding and responding to what its clients value, the more it will do 'well' within the marketplace.

So, where does the value in a given product actually lie? A company might have the best product on the market, but it will be unable to sell it if customers don't want it. On the other hand, when customers do want a product, it doesn't necessarily follow that they can afford it, or that they feel it is worth paying for.

Linked to this is the customer experience. This journey takes in the ease with which a customer can access a product, the quality of the product they receive, and the product's continued availability over time. It also encompasses how customers value various product features, and the emotional payoff or achievement involved in using the product: in other words, what they liked about the product, and how using it made them feel. Where customers are satisfied with the entire transactional experience surrounding a product, they are more likely to buy that product again. This is important, because success within the marketplace hinges not only on current demand, but also on the ability to attract and retain customers over the long term.

Up to this point, we have described the challenges facing any commercial enterprise. To a large extent, the same holds true for social enterprises. Market demand is clearly important. If clients can't or won't buy our products, or won't buy them again, the model fails. That said, social enterprises are about more than just doing well in the marketplace. 'Doing good' means thinking through three key issues: moving beyond demand and meeting needs, ensuring access to our products and services and balancing the needs of different groups of clients.

Meeting needs as well as wants

What we find notable about AMK is that its work is rooted in a deep and deliberate understanding not just of clients' *wants* but of clients' *needs*. It doesn't simply ask what clients like and can afford; it interrogates the opportunities and underlying constraints present in clients' uniquely vulnerable lives and livelihoods. It then uses this understanding to shape its products and services

http://dx.doi.org/10.3362/9781780448640.002

in a way that can potentially help clients to grasp those opportunities, and overcome challenges along the way. Importantly, these needs may be expressed or unexpressed – the latter set of needs particularly distinguish them from more easily identifiable 'market wants'.

However, it is also true that tensions often arise between meeting clients' wants and meeting their needs – especially where clients can't express those social needs themselves. For example, when we look at AMK's experience, we see examples of product characteristics driven by its focus on social value (meeting needs) that conflict with those driven by a responsiveness to client wants. Clients might buy our products (and even buy them again), but this doesn't necessarily mean that we can create real change, or as much change as we'd like to. This is because the needs of some clients might exceed their ability or willingness to pay. In other instances, there may be more demand for a different product that has less social value (or may even be harmful), or it may be that design elements that increase social value do not make the product more attractive to clients. For instance, AMK's detailed loan appraisal process serves to avoid over-indebting clients and minimize risk to AMK, but it adds effort and complexity to the process for the client. In this way, our challenge as social purpose organizations is to offer products that simultaneously satisfy clients' wants and address their underlying needs – because this is the most effective way of pulling a beneficial product through a market-led system.

Ensuring access

We've talked about the issue of access from a business perspective, but it looks slightly different from a doing good perspective. While thoughtful, needs-based design should translate into appropriate products, simply making that product available in the marketplace does not automatically mean that target clients can access it. Affordability, product features, location and timing of product delivery, and community or personal attitudes or perceptions can all serve to prevent target clients from accessing a product. Poorer people, or those living in more remote areas, may stand to benefit most from a particular service, but they may be less willing or able to pay for that service than others who are less marginalized. The point is, we need to think about who we are trying to reach, and ensure that our approach to design and delivery doesn't prevent us from doing so. For AMK, tackling access barriers meant getting out into rural areas where poor people lived, giving them small loans that they could afford and fitted with their cash-flows, and using poverty measurement to ensure that it was staying on track with its client targeting.

Balancing the needs of different groups

The final issue we need to grapple with is the diversity of needs among those we seek to serve. As we strive to understand the unique opportunities and vulnerabilities that characterize the lives of different groups of clients, the challenge is to design products and services that, as far as possible, respond to individual needs without disadvantaging any one group of clients by responding better to the needs of another. This is especially true when we use client feedback to improve our products and services – we need to make sure that we're hearing the voices of different groups, rather than just the loudest.

For AMK, understanding what its clients needed set the organization on a radically different path from that followed by many of its peers (both in Cambodia and internationally). By way of context: AMK was born in the heyday of expansion of the global microfinance industry, with many new entrants in the marketplace gaining a quick foothold by replicating a standard set of products and delivery channels offered by those already up and running (generally, non-collateralized loans delivered through groups of clients who guaranteed each other's loans). On the one hand, the spread of 'replicator' programmes facilitated the rapid expansion of financial services to the previously 'unbanked'. On the other hand, this tendency exposed the microfinance industry to the criticism that a one-size-fits-all approach overlooked the unique needs of poor clients in different contexts and (more worryingly) exposed those clients to potential harm through inappropriate products.

On a national level, Cambodia presented the ideal untapped market. In 2003 the country's economy was poised to enter a period of sustained economic growth that was to continue until the global economic crisis in 2008. This created both the demand for credit for investment in agriculture and small enterprises, and the resulting income by which clients could repay loans. There was also *room* to grow: in 2003, the top eight microfinance organizations in Cambodia together reached fewer than 240,000 clients (compared to over 1.4 million today). A supportive regulatory environment and an open attitude to foreign investment made Cambodia attractive to the burgeoning social investment market, and enabled charity microfinance programmes that were newly transformed into for-profit entities[1] to mobilize the capital needed to expand their businesses. Indeed, a 2013 report published by Micro-Credit Ratings International Ltd (M-CRIL) notes that from 2003 until the financial crisis hit in 2008, Cambodia was one of the fastest-growing microfinance markets in the world. This backdrop lends an interesting perspective to AMK's strategy.

Market demand *clearly* existed, and a number of organizations were gearing up to meet it. However, rather than simply responding to demand, AMK focused on addressing social needs. This took it into markets where no one else was operating (namely remote rural areas), and with products that no one else was offering (and that were designed to support clients' needs and protect them from harm) rather than the standard set of replicator products.

Why is all of this important? Shaping our business models around needs, rather than demand, matters for everyone involved – and the complexities of these factors evolve over a longer timeframe than those in a purely demand-driven model. Social enterprises operate at the nexus of value for clients and value for businesses. So when our products respond to the specific needs (and vulnerabilities) of clients, those clients can only benefit. Well-adapted products also put clients at lower risk of failure, which in turn reduces the risk for the organization investing in poor and vulnerable communities. The right products also generate loyalty. Especially where customers can choose between providers, the *better* product wins in the marketplace – and loyal clients potentially turn into repeat clients. In the case of AMK, getting clients back through the door after they've repaid their loan is important – not because the aim is to keep them in a state of perpetual debt, but because the changes that AMK seeks to create in their lives are part of a long-term process. And, as we will explore in Part III, client loyalty is an important part of building a sustainable business model: repeat clients cost less to serve. Setting up operations in a new area, recruiting and training new clients, and disbursing small loans are all investment costs that are only recuperated over the medium term.

A deliberate focus on social value creation and avoiding harm also helps us prevent stories like Seila's from ever happening – stories that can only damage the reputation of the social enterprise sector, and with it the long term viability of the business model. This is especially critical when seeking support from social investors to advance our work. In recent years, more and more stories have featured prominently in global and national news outlets. But, rather than discuss the potential of microfinance to create positive change, these have tended to highlight worrying instances of debt-related client suicide, mass client protests against microfinance providers, and an increasing tendency for national governments and the general public to view the entire movement with suspicion. Cambodia is not immune to critical headlines; for example a headline in the *Phnom Penh Post* in 2012 proclaimed 'Flood-affected poor "drowning in debt"'. In this context, AMK has noted the goodwill it generated among clients by introducing low-interest flood recovery loans to help those affected get back on their feet.

From a purely commercial perspective, AMK's focus on social value has helped it to differentiate itself in the marketplace. Its value-driven approach to product design has led AMK to see business opportunities it might not have seen otherwise, and to offer unique products to a (rural) set of clients different from that targeted by other providers, which gives the business a crucial competitive advantage (we'll learn about some of these innovations shortly). In a competitive marketplace such as Cambodia, this is all the more important.

The chapters in Part I explore how social enterprises can start becoming 'organizations for good' by shedding their assumptions about clients. In doing so, we'll look at how we can get to grips with what clients really need, rather than what we assume they want. AMK started by analysing clients' livelihoods to create its own product solution, rather than taking for granted that the standard set of replicator products offered by other providers was sufficient. Next, we'll look at how we can use this needs-based approach to guide us in improving our products and services over time. This will allow us to move beyond client satisfaction feedback and market research to understand what actually works, for whom, and above all, to have good conversations that get to the heart of what we are trying to do to create value for our clients.

CHAPTER 1

Insight: Don't just offer products; respond to client needs

Five years ago, I was heavily pregnant with my second child. The sun had not yet risen when I realized that I was bleeding heavily. I remember how my heart sank when the village midwife told me that I needed to go to the provincial hospital for an emergency caesarean section. Welcoming a baby into this world is supposed to be a happy event, but without the $50 I needed for the operation, I feared for the worst. I knew they wouldn't even let me enter the hospital, let alone see a doctor. What could I do? As the contractions became more regular, all I could hear was the midwife's warning in my mind: 'You'll lose your baby, and your little girl might lose her mother too.' My family couldn't help me with the money but fortunately the neighbour, who had heard the commotion, came to the door. She was the president of our village bank, and reminded me that I could get an emergency loan from AMK. I had been in the group for more than six months, so I could apply. She lent me her phone, and even dialled the numbers because my hands were shaking so much. When I talked to the client officer, I couldn't believe what he was saying to me. I could have the loan. I didn't need to travel to the branch, I didn't even need to fill out any papers. He just said: 'Go to the hospital now. I'll meet you there with the money. The paperwork can wait.' And so I did. I still remember that somehow, that day, the distance between my village and the hospital in town had doubled – every bump on that long road caused me pain. I was in agony – but I was also full of hope and amazement at what had just happened. I wasn't going to lose my baby after all. It seemed like a dream. But sure enough, an hour later, I met the client officer on the steps of the hospital. He told me that he had already paid the money, and that they were waiting for me inside. And do you know? The client officer came back the next day, to visit me and my beautiful new son. He was as proud as any uncle – and his eyes just shone when I told him that I decided to name my son 'AMK'.

Samnang (AMK client)

Here we have a story of a microfinance client in a desperate situation, and an organization that supported her when she needed it most, at precisely the right time and in the right way. From a client perspective, the emergency loan is a great product. Loans of up to the equivalent of $100 (with a 10-month term) are disbursed within *four hours* of being requested, and often the client officer will deliver the money to wherever the client happens to be at the time. The paperwork is handled at a later date, only one guarantor is needed (and this too is sorted out afterwards), and during the loan term only interest repayments apply (charged at a lower rate than AMK's other products). What we also find notable about this story is the business value that the emergency loan represents: introduced in 2005, it is a product that was then (and still is) unique to AMK, and which enables AMK to clearly distinguish itself in a crowded marketplace. From an institutional perspective, the emergency loan is potentially risky, at least on paper. AMK lets funds go out the door quickly, with no up-front checks, for less profit, and with fewer guarantees than it requires for its other products. On the other hand, AMK defines 'emergency' quite narrowly (health or family funeral expenses), which acts to limit its portfolio exposure. In fact, AMK's experience is that although this product accounts for less than 1 per cent of its books, clients consistently cite it as a cause for satisfaction with AMK's work. That is, even if they don't use it very often, clients feel secure knowing it's available when they need it.

However, the most interesting part of the story isn't the loan itself, or even the benefit to the client. Of *most* interest is what came before Samnang's tale even began: the steps that led AMK to understand the challenges faced by its clients, and to design an appropriate response. So how did it do it? It began by throwing out its assumptions about clients and, instead, sought to find out who its clients were, what was really happening in their lives, and what it was they really needed to improve their lives.

Why making assumptions is bad for clients and bad for business

We've talked about why, for social enterprises, a needs-based (rather than market-based) approach is good for clients and institutions alike. But underlying this is a fundamental question around how we get to the place where we understand those needs. This is worth asking because it's all too easy to make assumptions, and for organizations trying to do good in the world, assumptions are actually quite dangerous. They can lead us to offer thoughtful products where there is no market, or to offer the wrong solution where there is a market. They also expose our operations to reality gaps: situations where staff apply our products in a way other than we had intended, to try and better meet clients' needs. While this might work in the short term, there's a danger that some of the 'value' built into our products is being distorted on the ground. Not only can assumptions steer us away from doing good, they can also do harm to the very clients we seek to serve. For example, it's common practice to assume that clients can make monthly repayments, but this is problematic for those whose income comes in less frequently, such as in the wake of the annual harvest. In this way, assumptions are bad for clients and bad for business.

This might sound like a radical (and complex) approach, but there's a real history to AMK's 'no assumptions' mindset. This history was described poignantly as we talked with Theresa McDonnell Friström, the Concern Cambodia Country Director between 2002 and 2005 (and former chair of AMK's Board):

What became clear to me was that despite trying to help our clients, we didn't really understand their needs and living conditions. I recall the day that the finance manager walked into my office with bad news. After two years of devastating floods, bad debts in one branch were double what we had anticipated them to be – totalling $75,000. My immediate instinct was to write off the bad loans. I felt if countries can write off debt, why can't we do the same for poor people who are vulnerable to natural disaster? My idea, however, met with unexpected resistance. Management staff convinced me that we should visit the villages and get a sense of what was really happening with clients. The results, I must say, really shocked me. In only three villages were clients genuinely unable to repay; clients in the other six villages were able but merely unwilling, and using the flood as an excuse not to repay. Could we really afford to not understand our clients' lives? No sooner was this behind us than we found instances of staff fraud. To achieve their poverty targets, client officers were creating 'ghost clients', using the names of the poorest households on the loan applications – but then taking the loans for their own use and putting clients under pressure to repay loans that they never received. How is it that we were hurting the very people we were trying to help? I believed, and still do, that people should not be worse off as a result of our development initiatives. For this to happen, it's clear that our work needs to be rooted in a deep understanding of clients' needs, and we need to recognize the potential of quite serious harm we could cause clients as a result of poorly designed and managed systems.

In light of these experiences, one of the critical lessons from the Concern Programme (which resonated with many members of the new AMK Board) was that making assumptions was to be avoided at all costs. The new organization needed to invest in understanding its clients' lives and livelihoods, and translate this understanding into meaningful strategic and operational decisions around what to offer, and how. Having decided to take nothing about its clients for granted, AMK took the (comparatively unusual) decision to invest heavily in an in-house research department from the outset. Indeed, the research manager was the first new hire – appointed even before the first CEO was in place. Research in those early days was focused around finding out what AMK already knew about its clients, and fleshing out that picture through sample-based investigation (and feedback from field staff) to build up a picture of the characteristics and needs of different client groups. This covered everything from household composition and construction to food intake, income sources, levels of assets and debt, and expenditure patterns.

Understanding client livelihoods

So who were AMK's clients, precisely? In 2003, the majority of people AMK served (most of whom were women) were involved in rural agriculture – specifically rain-fed rice production. Rice is the centrepiece of the Cambodian economic landscape and diet, with rice production accounting for 84 per cent of cultivated land. It dominates agricultural labour and output, as well as the Cambodian diet, accounting for 68 per cent of the daily caloric intake of the average Cambodian adult.[2] The national importance of this foodstuff is woven into the very fabric of Cambodia's language; the Khmer for 'to eat' translates literally as 'eat rice' (*pisa bei*). Rice production is labour-intensive work, requiring considerable attention to precise paddy preparation, water-level management, delicate weeding and constant pest control to produce a successful harvest. Wet-rice labour inputs are concentrated in the nine-month rainy season between May and January, with peaks of intensity occurring in May (for land preparation), June–July (for transplanting seedlings), and November–December (for harvesting).

AMK understood, however, that it needed to move beyond a superficial scan of 'what our clients do to earn a living', and get to grips with the financial realities of those livelihoods: the extent (or lack) of diversity in terms of household income sources; what levels of income clients generally expect to see; the nature of how this income fluctuates over the course of the typical year; and when cash-flow 'crunch points' emerge (whether these be from coping with health emergencies or disaster, or from more predictable life-cycle events such as weddings or festivals). Crucially, AMK also sought to understand how the livelihoods and vulnerabilities of various client groups differed – for example, clients involved in agricultural production as opposed to those involved in small trading or labouring work.

AMK's initial research findings turned the common perception of rural clients neatly on its head: namely that clients weren't singularly dependent on agricultural income to survive. They clearly had mixed economic baskets: while nearly all rural households (99 per cent) engaged in at least one traditional 'farm' activity (which accounted for about one third of household income), 96 per cent of clients also counted on non-farm work (such as tailoring or carpentry) to provide income. Moreover, 79 per cent had other income streams – often from children working in the burgeoning garment factories, which by 2003 contributed 15 per cent of GDP, as well as from those working in construction, which accounted for 6 per cent of GDP (as illustrated by Chandararot and Ballard's 2004 Cambodia Annual Economic review). Looking at the seasonality and volatility of cash-flow patterns generated another interesting finding. When AMK asked clients to name the months when they most needed to borrow, there was a clear concentration of answers in the period from May to September, coinciding with the paddy preparation and seedling transplanting phases (rather than the post-harvest period of January to April, as AMK might have assumed). Interrogating household consumption patterns revealed that clients need access to funds throughout the year, not just during the planting season. This includes paying for religious ceremonies, building enterprise and household assets, school fees and health expenses. Where poor people don't have cash to hand when they need to invest or cover expenses, then (in the absence of access to credit), they are forced to sell assets or curtail their food consumption.

Designing products that respond to needs

AMK's research helped it build up a picture of its clients' livelihoods – which are varied, uncertain, and vulnerable to shocks (such as crop failure or emergencies). It brought this knowledge to bear in designing products and services aimed at helping clients harness economic opportunities and avoid the pitfalls associated with debt. In practice, this entailed a decisive move away from the typical standardized approach and towards a product design that gives clients access to the right amount of credit when they think they need it; for the right length of time, in line with their livelihood; and which builds in time for them to recover from unexpected shocks, such as crop failure, before the loan falls due. AMK also helps clients manage risk by providing other financial services (such as savings and insurance), and building flexibility into its products. As we'll learn, some of the choices it made were quite radical, not just within the Cambodian microfinance market but compared to what was then considered international best practice.

Enabling clients to take good decisions

When we say that AMK is 'risk-aware', we don't mean that it simply manages risk on behalf of its clients. Yes, it does all it can upfront to protect and support clients, but it also gives them the space they need to manage their own risk. For example, soon after AMK's registration (as a separate entity rather than a programme run by the charity Concern), its Management took the interesting decision to drop the loan utilization checks that were part of Concern's methodology. Why so? Let's revisit some basics here. Microfinance investment loans aim to help clients improve their economic situation (in the long term) through engaging in more (or more effective) income-generating activities (in the short term). Ideally, this means that clients will invest their loans in their enterprise – whether this is in the form of agriculture, trading or production. Within this framework (or so the theory goes), using microloans for consumption purposes (for example, buying a cooking stove for the household, or food for the family) creates a drag effect on clients' potential return on investment. When this happens, clients miss out on the opportunity to optimize their income, which in turn can hinder their capacity to repay their loan with interest (which is problematic for both client and lender). From this perspective, checking whether clients are actually using the loan to invest in their business is important.

AMK's take on this situation differs somewhat. There exists a line of argument that clients themselves are best placed to plan and execute decisions about how to use their money. For example, using a portion of an enterprise loan to buy a cooking stove for the home is, from the lender's perspective, a textbook case of diverting a business loan for consumption. But let's consider carefully the role of the cooking stove in the life of the client: if it is a labour-saving (therefore time-saving) device, does it not free up the client to devote more attention to business activities? And what if the client uses part of a business loan to buy medicine for a serious, unexpected illness? Essentially, here we have a client using available money to solve a health problem; an investment which potentially stands to generate higher returns than buying stock that she is unable to sell because she is unwell.

Shaping the path, not driving the car

AMK believes that its role in helping clients make good decisions is to shape the financial path, rather than drive the car. It uses cash-flow analysis to design the broad parameters of the lending relationship: how much, for how long, and at what interest rate. It also uses its contact with clients in training and group meetings to emphasize the value of investment. And that's where it stops. As AMK Board member Rebecca McKenzie reflects, it's about allowing clients the dignity of choosing what they want to do with their money, and recognizing that, owing to rapidly changing client economies, flexibility helps clients take advantage of new opportunities and successfully navigate the bumps in the road.

Loan utilization, therefore, is a data point that is monitored, but not supervised. AMK's Management knows that approximately 30 per cent of loan capital is used for consumption purposes, and it is comfortable with this level given its stability over time. (Were Management to see an increasing trend in the future, this would prompt further research and a conversation about the most appropriate response.) To some, 30 per cent might seem like a high rate of 'loan leak', but for AMK, it is simply a recognition that clients' financial needs are frequent and varied, and is built into the assumptions about affordability in the loan application process. AMK's point is this: when such needs arise (and when access to formal credit is lacking), clients will either curtail consumption, or borrow from informal sources (and at higher interest rates, if the loan is from the local money-lender) to cover them. From AMK's perspective, neither of these options is good enough.

Helping clients meet their investment needs

So, we've learned about how AMK creates flexibility to allow clients to use a portion of their loans for non-investment purposes. But what about making good business investments? Without a detailed picture of the realities of clients' lives, the obvious choice (from a product design perspective) might simply be to go into rural areas and offer a typical group loan. By the time AMK started up, most microfinance organizations in Cambodia had moved beyond the common international practice of issuing loans paid in weekly or monthly instalments. These loans can work for clients with an enterprise that generates regular turnover, but those clients investing in agriculture need a lump-sum input at one certain time of the year, which can be repaid (also in a lump sum) using income generated by the harvest later in the year.

AMK inherited a group loan product from Concern that featured end-of-term repayment of principal (with interest paid monthly). So far, so good. But as we've discussed, AMK's research highlighted that clients had income streams other than agriculture. This did not mean, however, that they were able to cope with regular instalments; their income sources might have been varied, but they were also volatile. When AMK added all this up, it realized that simply basing repayment schedules on the agricultural season did not allow clients the flexibility to access loans and to repay them when they were most able to; complete financial flexibility was key. For this reason, AMK changed the loan terms to allow clients to repay the end-of-term loan at any point within the cycle, with no penalties for pre-payment. Not only that, but AMK also responded to the income volatility question (particularly the risk of crop failure) with a flexible credit line product that spread risk over more than one growing season (see Box 'The credit line product').

From AMK's point of view, offering the credit line product was a highly risky strategy (and indeed the idea caused jitters from Board level down – in fact some client officers are still resistant to the idea). Would clients borrow too much? Would they pay back at all? What would it mean for the institution's own cash-flow if clients were drawing down different amounts at different times, and repaying when it suited them? Looking across the marketplace at the time, other financial service providers were vigorously competing to attract new customers by offering increasingly large loans. AMK's choice was different: it understood (both from a needs perspective and an 'avoiding harm' perspective) that better loans were needed, not larger ones. And by 'better', AMK meant the right amount of credit, at the right time, for the right length of time.

If group loan clients could prove they had sufficient income streams, they could apply for such a loan (initially Management restricted eligibility for this product to a client's third successful loan cycle, as an incentive for good repayment performance). To manage the risk of this higher-volume, longer-term product, AMK relied on its in-depth knowledge of, and connection to, its clients; it looked at repayment history, and drew on its presence in the villages and the home-based loan assessment procedure. For most other providers, their only

---

The credit line product

In 2005, AMK launched a unique credit line product that handed clients complete control over the loan: size (up to a ceiling initially the equivalent of $125, the same as the group loan); the ability to draw down the loan in instalments, ensuring that money will be available exactly when clients need it (which means they are only paying interest on money when they actually need it); and the scope to determine their own repayment schedule. By providing a 24-month loan term (as opposed to the 12-month group loan term), AMK gave clients the ability to spread risk over multiple growing seasons, rather than making successful repayment reliant on the vagaries of a single harvest.

interaction with clients was branch-based. After several years of experience with the product, AMK realized that credit line drawdowns were largely predictable, effectively following the agricultural cycle, so the fear that the loan would cause liquidity problems was unfounded. Moreover, its tracking data revealed that repayment rates for the credit line product were actually *higher* than repayment rates for the supposedly safer instalment loan products (especially during the financial crisis). By 2010, AMK's Management realized that client satisfaction with the credit line product exceeded that generated by other products. This, coupled with higher exit rates in early cycles for other products, prompted AMK to extend credit line eligibility to second-cycle clients.

While the credit line product aimed to provide better, more flexible credit (rather than just more credit), one question remained. What about clients who did actually need larger loans? Clearly, as clients completed more and more loan cycles, their economic basket would increase, and they would eventually 'outgrow' the small group loan sizes. Recognizing this, in 2004 AMK launched an individual loan product which gave clients access to larger loans. These were targeted only at those households that had regular income streams, and AMK insisted that they should be repaid in regular instalments, rather than through the end-of-term 'balloon' payment featured in their group loans. The rationale was this: money repaid regularly translated into a steady income stream for AMK, and allowed it to spot problems as they arose rather than waiting until the end of the loan term to discover that the client might struggle to repay.

AMK's first individual loan product

The individual loan products featured higher loan ceilings than the group loan (up to the equivalent of $250 for the first loan, and $500 from the second cycle). Where group loan clients had regular income streams, and could provide two guarantors (and a collateral guarantee), they could 'graduate' to this new product as their businesses grew.

The challenge of living on one dollar a day is that it's just an average

The challenge that poor people face is not just that their income is small, but that it is unpredictable. We talk about poor people living on 'a dollar a day', but this label masks the simple truth: that this number is only an average. Some days people have a little more, some days they have a little less, and some days they have nothing. Talking with poor people, the most common issue they raise is that they don't know whether there will be money to feed the family on any given day. Beyond this, having money to pay for predictable expenditure (such as school fees) is also a challenge. But it's not just their income that is unpredictable, it's also the demands on that income: occasional accidents or illnesses arise that require money to overcome. AMK understood the uncertainty of its clients' lives, and shaped its products to help them invest in the face of that uncertainty. What, then, is the role of financial services in helping clients respond to emergencies, or to manage income fluctuations so as to meet regular payments (such as utilities or school fees), or one-off expenditures (such as ceremonies, weddings or births)? Let's go back to the research for a moment.

In 2004, a clear message emerged from AMK's research: clients' lives are punctuated with devastating shocks that affect their ability to earn an income, or that tax their ability to cope financially. Cambodian agriculture (particularly rice production) depends entirely on the timeliness and adequacy of the monsoons. It is labour-intensive work, involving the whole family, but all that human input will come to naught without the right amount of rain at the right time, as AMK's own Tanmay Chetan reflected in the *Small Enterprise Development Journal* in 2007. Beyond the very real vagaries of nature, AMK's research highlighted that 80 per cent of clients experience a health crisis or accident on an annual basis. As you might expect, vulnerability to health shocks (as opposed to droughts and floods) does not vary significantly between regions and enterprise types – all clients were equally subject to setbacks. And let's not forget: for a client in crisis, needing to repay a debt only adds to the strain of recovery.

Armed with these insights, AMK wanted to understand what safety nets clients had created for themselves. But first let's consider the anatomy of a crisis. A shock happens, which is unforeseen. Overcoming these shocks – whether they relate to a client's health, wellbeing or business – requires immediate access to a relatively large lump sum of cash. Money solves problems. It buys medicine or hospital care, replaces stolen inventory, repairs a broken asset, or purchases additional ones. So, AMK wished to know, were clients able to access such lump sums when they needed them? What were their coping mechanisms?

AMK's research revealed that contrary to popular belief, the poor had a genuine ability (and tendency) to save; in fact, only 10 per cent of clients were unable to save. What clients did *not* do, however, was to save in formal financial institutions, or to save large amounts at regular intervals. Rather, they held small amounts of non-monetary savings in the form of tangible assets (such as gold or livestock) at one specific time of year (after the harvest season, when they enjoyed excess liquidity). These savings were, however, both insecure (i.e. susceptible to depreciation through loss, theft, or shifts in prices) and often costly (where clients couldn't access them quickly when needed). Conventional wisdom also holds that a key coping mechanism used by poor people facing a 'cash crunch' is to reduce the quality or quantity of food – essentially, to go on a crisis diet (which of course is problematic for a range of reasons, not least because of the health implications, which often affect clients' productivity). In this regard, AMK's research revealed that nearly one quarter of new clients faced regular or occasional hunger. It found that in emergencies, poor people also resorted to taking on debt, often from a local money-lender (a costly coping mechanism, given the generally high interest rates charged). Given the shortcomings inherent in all of these coping mechanisms, AMK set about exploring what it could do to strengthen them.

Planning for the expected, and coping with the unexpected

Savings – often referred to as the 'forgotten half of microfinance' – play a key role in planning and coping. A savings 'safety net' is an important source of ready cash to cope with emergencies and to cover both unexpected and anticipated day-to-day and life-cycle expenses. The savings and credit programme run by Concern, which was the precursor to AMK, included a feature called an 'internal fund', which is common in organizations using the village bank methodology (originally developed in Latin America). Clients' voluntary savings were held in a secure safe by the village bank committee (headed by the village bank president), and Concern staff managed the record-keeping. This fund could be lent to village bank members in addition to their normal loans from AMK. However, AMK saw that, in reality, the fund was problematic on a number of levels. Firstly, it was a costly and complex approach to savings mobilization, given the need for high levels of coordination between the client officer and the village bank committee (a strain on productivity). Moreover, it was hard to determine the payoff for this level of effort. As the village banks managed their own funds, client officers often lacked access to information on how those funds were being managed and used.

Secondly, and more worryingly, the fund was susceptible to corruption and monopolization by the village bank president – as illustrated in the Prologue – particularly given the domination of this position by village chiefs. Some context is useful here. Cambodia's social and political history had effectively destroyed community solidarity and trust. In those years of a nascent democracy, when AMK was created, authority was highly centralized, including at the level of the village chief. While the village bank committee was technically in charge of deciding how to distribute these savings to members (in the form of loans), the village chief (who generally acted as president) held a lot of sway in terms of decision-making. This resulted in cases of misappropriation of savings, preferential lending to friends and relatives of the village bank president, and a general decline in overall financial discipline in the village bank. (We'll discuss in Chapter 4 how AMK tackled the problem of village chiefs holding the village bank president function).

Given that AMK was unable to measure the benefits, and in recognition of the very real possibility of corruption (and the moral hazard this presented the organization), the internal fund was scrapped. Having done away with it, AMK developed an individual savings product, managed by AMK and accessed through the monthly group meetings. That having been said, a lack of client trust in savings, and the fact that clients were either limited to making deposits and withdrawals once per month (at meetings), or had to travel long distances to the branch office to carry out transactions more frequently, meant that between 2004 and 2009, less than 2,000 clients actually opened an account – and those that did saved only very small amounts (averaging less than $10).

AMK has always seen itself as a financial service provider rather than simply a loan company, even though until recently its offering has been dominated by credit. Since the earliest days, when AMK experimented with an insurance product (which was, at the time, blocked by regulation), it has sought to provide financial products for non-investment needs. Emergency loans partly filled the gap left by the lack of an insurance product in helping clients deal with unexpected shocks. More recently, as technology has improved and regulatory barriers have been lifted, AMK has started to offer a broader range of services that help clients manage risk. These include savings schemes accessible at village level using local agents, microinsurance covering health and accidents, and transfer services (to facilitate the movement of money within families and their broader financial networks when needed). These products work both from a client perspective (in terms of providing value) and an institutional perspective (because they allow AMK to diversify and reduce risk in the face of an increasingly saturated credit market in some parts of the country). They are covered in more depth in Chapter 6.

Designing products to avoid harm

If flexible investment and savings tools can help clients cope with the uncertainty, seasonality and volatility of their livelihoods, then AMK has positioned itself to deliver real social value to clients. But what about the question of harm? Loans are debts, after all – which can make poor people *more* vulnerable than ever within their uncertain lives. How, then, has AMK minimized the potential that microfinance has to inflict real damage on clients and their communities?

AMK recognizes that the reality of the lives of poor people means that the risk of failure is high, whether this is through borrowing beyond their capacity to repay, failure of an investment, or as a result of the impact of a shock such as ill health or natural disaster. The organization therefore places huge importance on understanding (and reducing the impact of) the risks faced by clients, particularly in relation to their borrowing.

In as much as AMK assumes implicit and explicit responsibility for delivering value and avoiding harm, its model implies a contract with clients that is more than simply transactional. In this way, the understanding of value and harm that AMK seeks is not merely an academic (or public relations) exercise; the question of 'what does this decision mean for clients?' is central to the strategic and operational thinking of the organization. In practice, this leads AMK to identify risk factors inherent in its business model (for both the client and the institution) and to design its products and services in a way that avoids harm (to counter, for example, the risk of over-indebtedness). So when we talk about the risk involved in borrowing, it's important to stress that we're talking about a client's entire debt picture. That is to say, AMK didn't start operating in a rural financial vacuum – its early client-level research revealed that more often than not, clients had loans from other informal sources (often local money-lenders, charging onerous interest rates). In this way, to the extent that AMK is able to *replace* its client's informal debt with its own debt – one that is designed to provide flexibility and protect against harm – it actually serves to reduce the overall risk to the client.

From a product design perspective, the first and most important priority for AMK is to ensure upfront that clients do not take on too much debt. For this reason, AMK insists that loan amounts should be decided upon completion of a cash-flow analysis for each client. This is conducted in the clients' home, so that the client officer can verify the applicant's living conditions, business assets, and other relevant factors. (In Chapter 3, we'll look at what went wrong with this aspect of AMK's product design, and how the organization got back on track). Loan size ceilings also have an important role to play, not just in terms of poverty targeting, but in avoiding over-indebtedness – we'll tackle this issue in greater depth in Chapter 5.

At a delivery methodology level, AMK's commitment to creating value and avoiding harm can be seen in its decision to fix the problems associated with village bank presidents, rather than abandon this important aspect of the methodology as many competitors have done. What are the benefits of this approach? Firstly, village bank presidents help leverage local knowledge to ensure that the right people are joining the groups and that they are given loans that they can handle. They also bring knowledge about clients' situations and local factors that might create risk for borrowers or help resolve problems. Staff agree that, given that client officer caseloads have risen as high as 937, the village bank president plays a critical burden-sharing role in the staff-client relationship. In such cases, where staff need to work efficiently and spend less time with each individual client, the clients still get the support they need.

Recognizing both the risks and potential rewards involved in this aspect of its methodology, AMK sought the middle ground to make this role work. It instituted a policy of elections and term limits for village bank presidents. It also brought gender equality to the composition of the group management: where the president was a man, the deputy president had to be a woman, and

---

The role of the village bank president

At a village level, AMK clients form small solidarity lending groups[3] of three to six members, and 20 groups unite to form a village bank. At the head of this standard operating unit sits the village bank president, who provides an important link between the clients in a village bank and AMK client officers.

The president helps each member fill out his/her loan application form, and later provides feedback on the credit-worthiness of each applicant to the credit officer. The village bank president also undertakes an important problem-solving function in cases where clients find themselves struggling with repayments and need business advice.

vice versa. The village chief, and members of his immediate family, were barred from running (although in practice, owing to the need for the president to be literate, some 15 per cent of elected presidents are in fact still chiefs). Within the Cambodian context of the day, this was a radical decision: among AMK's four main competitors, two had dropped the president role entirely, and the remaining two were still relying on the village chief.

Supporting clients when things go wrong

Up-front design and methodology considerations, such as tailoring loan sizes based on individual repayment capacity, are a good starting point in ensuring that a client does not become over-indebted. But what happens *after* a loan has been given also matters – a lot. So what can be done when things go wrong for clients?

The first interesting choice that AMK made to protect clients was to wipe the 'debt slate' clean when required, by introducing a death write-off policy unique in the marketplace. The policy is well used, with current write-off of around 100 clients per month (around 0.4 per cent of the portfolio per year). This is not insignificant when considering that AMK's bad debt rate is mostly below 0.2 per cent, but is seen as a valuable policy for attracting and retaining clients.

Collecting blood from a snail

A well-known Khmer proverb discusses the impossibility of extracting blood from a snail: they simply have none to give.[4] This old adage is relevant to a story involving a client who died, a client officer who accidentally stumbled upon a funeral, an irate local politician, and an interesting institutional response. Bear in mind that debt is a risk for clients, and individual risk gets promoted to 'family risk' when a client dies and that client's relatives are required to pay off the loan. This is what happened: in 2005, unbeknownst to AMK, a client that had taken out an individual loan suddenly died. The client officer visited the village in the course of his routine loan collection rounds, and happened upon the seventh-day funeral, already underway. To his client, upon realizing what was happening, he decided not to collect the repayment instalment, and instead pay his respects to the family and offer to contribute some money towards the cost of the ceremony. However, a guest at the ceremony of some political standing became irate, accusing AMK of 'trying to collect blood from a snail'. The guest took the story to the local media, framing AMK as a predatory organization and demanding loan forgiveness. This was an important 'light bulb' moment for AMK in terms of understanding its clients' needs. In response, it introduced a general policy of loan write-off in the case of death of a client, to avoid putting the client's family in harm's way.

The second interesting choice that AMK made related to clients who *were* able to repay their loans – but not at that moment. From a financial service provider perspective, it's clearly important that clients repay their loans lest the institution start haemorrhaging capital. Indeed, historically and at a global sector level, a lot of positive noise has been made about the high repayment rates achieved by microfinance organizations (in some developing countries, banks for poor people even have lower portfolio-at-risk rates than those for people in the middle and upper income brackets). However, without a detailed understanding of how each institution works with clients at risk of default, it is difficult to generalize. Are high repayment rates a sign of well-designed, well-managed products for the right clients, or the end result of harsh collection practices? Microfinance collection policies often stipulate that clients in distress receive a given number of visits by increasingly senior staff before collateral seizure or court proceedings. In line with its commitment to client protection, however, AMK implements what is known as a 'soft collections practice'. This does not mean that AMK is soft on its clients' responsibility to repay, but it does distinguish between clients who *can't* pay and clients who *won't* pay. The latter are vigorously pursued for their repayments, through phone calls, visits, and conversations with neighbours and family. Where, on the other hand, clients express a genuine willingness, but an inability, to repay, AMK works with them to find a solution to the problem, and to get the client on the road to recovery, rather than simply covering its own liabilities and leaving the client to flounder. Staff are trained to visit clients and their group, to try and understand the root cause of default, and work to find a solution; there is provision for rescheduling loans, for example. In fact, clients can only be taken to court to seize collateral with AMK Board approval. To date only one case has been referred to Board level, and this did not result in court action. Contrast this with other MFIs, who often have in-house legal departments to deal with collateral execution.

Looking ahead

Shedding its assumptions about clients has enabled AMK to design a suite of products that help clients effectively grasp opportunities within their uniquely unpredictable lives, while reducing the likelihood that the benefits presented by access to credit will lead to over-indebtedness. Doing its homework on clients, and creating a tailored product line, has also helped AMK to distinguish itself in the marketplace, and move beyond market wants to create real social value. However, designing a product and bringing it to market is only the first consideration. Products also need to match the reality that operational staff experience on the ground. This hands-on delivery experience needs to feed into understanding how the product works in practice: whether adjustments are needed; whether it works for some clients and not others; and whether some aspects of design (while great in theory) are simply too hard to implement. This means being engaged at all levels (particularly through research, and operations and field staff) with the question of what is working for whom, to ensure that insights and lessons from the ground translate into improved practice. And this is precisely where the insight discussed in Chapter 2 becomes important.

CHAPTER 2

Insight: Ask good questions; have good conversations

'We want bigger loans.' That was essentially the main message coming from our clients. I remember it was 2006, and we'd just started doing client satisfaction surveys. To be honest, we'd heard the same from our field staff – they were always pushing Management on the fact that clients needed larger loans. But at Board level, there was ongoing concern that increasing loan sizes might result in a loss of focus. We were in the business of serving poor clients, and larger loans were potentially risky for everyone involved: for clients because it could possibly be too much debt, and for us if they couldn't actually pay them back. And now we were hearing the same feedback from our clients themselves – which was worrying, but it also sparked an interesting dialogue between the Research department and the Board.

Essentially, at that point, we had two choices: raise the maximum loan cap (while ensuring loans were still linked to capacity to repay), or keep it at the same level. We went back and forth about the risks and opportunities of each option – but it was really when we looked closer at the data that the right answer snapped into focus. As it so happened, when we segmented the data by poverty level, it was only a minority of our clients that were clamouring for larger loans – and those were the better-off clients in the groups. The poorer clients were actually happy with loan sizes. So we decided not to act on the feedback. I can well imagine that if we had been a purely market-driven business, we wouldn't have thought twice about raising the cap. But we focus on what's most important – serving poor clients – and we put every decision through this lens.

Howard Dalzell (AMK Board member
and chair of the Social Performance Committee)

In the last chapter, we talked about how AMK took a needs-driven approach to product design, rather than a demand-driven approach. AMK shed its assumptions and explored the realities of clients' lives, and used this to define effective ways of helping them grasp opportunities and overcome barriers. These are the steps that AMK took upfront to define how it engaged with its clients – however the process of understanding its clients didn't stop there. Once its products and services were out in the marketplace, the imperative shifted to finding out whether these were actually doing what they were supposed to do, and how to improve them.

It is accepted good practice for businesses to collect feedback from customers. For a purely commercial business, the questions are more or less straightforward. It's broadly a case of asking what customers liked and didn't like, or what would make them more likely to buy a product next time. But as social enterprises, we also need to find out how to make our products and services better at actually doing the good that we envisioned in our design. For this reason, we need to ask good questions. We need to find out what is working, and what is not, in terms of creating change in our clients' lives.

That said, the concept of 'good questions' involves a degree of nuance. It's not just about what's working (or not) – but *for whom*. As Howard Dalzell mentions above, small loan sizes have historically been a cornerstone of AMK's poverty outreach methodology, both in terms of encouraging clients to self-select into its programme, and making sure they were not overburdened with debt (we'll learn more about this in Chapter 5). But this is not to suggest that good design features automatically translate into good outcomes for *all clients*. Here's why. While a social enterprise should set out to design its product offering based on an informed view of a typical member of its target client group, the reality is more complex. Averages simply do not exist, and different clients will have a different experience of using the same product depending on a number of factors: their capabilities (skills, experience); their level of vulnerability (health, assets, family or community ties, or housing conditions); or even contextual factors (location, access to other services, presence of competition).

So, what happens if we don't ask good questions about what's working for whom? Firstly, we potentially miss opportunities to do more good where scope exists to improve our existing offering based on our clients' experiences. Secondly, if we fail to understand the experience of different groups of clients, then we risk taking the wrong decision in response to feedback. The danger is that we make decisions that help some clients, but hurt others. It's also important to recognize that often the least vulnerable or least marginalized clients will shout loudest about what they want. Keeping a focus on clients' needs, and on whose needs we are trying to meet, helps to cut through the noise of client feedback, allowing us to take decisions on how to improve our products and services in a way that fully supports our social goals.

Asking good questions

So what are good questions? As discussed in Chapter 1, AMK invested heavily in research from the outset – and its earliest questions focused around understanding 'who are our clients?' Its client profile information included questions on demographics, household income sources, expenditure sources, cash-flow patterns, asset levels, debt levels, and general levels of household vulnerability to shocks. The insights that it captured fed into product design that was tailored, appropriate, responsible and flexible – in line with the needs of its target group: poor rural Cambodians.

A key part of making this work was the formation of a Social Performance Committee (SPC) early in the development of the organization. In July 2005, the Board approved the formation of this committee, which brought together a diverse group of individuals: a University academic, a Cambodian rural development practitioner, a statistician, and a development consultant. Reporting to the Board, the SPC mirrors the functions of AMK's Audit and Finance Committee, and guides the organization in the development of a rigorous and practical system with the dual objective of ensuring adherence to its stated mission, and procuring reliable and relevant market information for internal decision-making. The aim was not to prove AMK's impact, but rather to help make the organization as good as it could be. In the early days, the SPC's focus was very much on bringing rigour to AMK's focus on reaching and serving poor people. To ensure that AMK was not making any assumptions about its clients, the SPC would review research questions, comment on the methodology, ensure the accuracy of data, manage issues relating to research quality, and help interpret data and the implications of research for the Board. In this way, it made sure that when the Research department asked questions about clients, it could be reasonably certain that it was asking *good* questions, was getting good data in response, and could understand the practical relevance of this data. In those early years, when products were being revamped (or introduced) in line with AMK's new and detailed understanding of clients' lives, this was an essential function.

With this initial picture of clients' lives in place, AMK's research priorities shifted with a view to exploring two further questions: 'what is actually happening with clients as a result of using our products?' (in comparison with initial baseline data); and, 'how can we serve our clients better/more fully?' (based on client feedback). This marked a shift away from in-depth client research towards more operationally focused research, analysis of performance data aimed at understanding client behaviour, and a general focus on how to improve AMK's work and develop new products. Given the organization's focus on serving poor clients, segmenting information by poverty status became a critical part of the data analysis phase. Specifically, segmenting client data (around who had left the programme, who was dissatisfied, whose poverty levels were not improving, etc.) based on poverty level, gender or enterprise type provided a richness to AMK's analysis that allowed it to make operationally useful decisions (see Figure 2.1).

Having good conversations

The point about ensuring that client-level insights feed into action is important, because it's easy to assume that the process is fairly automatic. Not so. As most researchers or evaluators would agree, high-quality research does not necessarily lead to tangible changes in how things are done on the ground. In our experience, organizations need to do three things well: understand clients and their needs (research); translate these insights into strategy; and

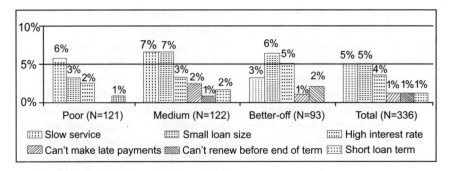

Figure 2.1 Client dissatisfaction by wellbeing category
Source: 2013 AMK client satisfaction report

reflect and learn as that strategy is implemented, in order to improve along the way.

... between Research and the Board

While interviewing both Management and Board members for this book, we often heard that AMK is a data-driven organization, and that its work is designed around evidence, rather than just intuition (or good intentions). AMK does high-quality, rigorous research, with the explicit objective of informing what it does as an organization – specifically to ensure that its understanding of clients continually shapes product design and improvement. This is notable, because the critical connection between these is often weak or missing entirely in other organizations.

Reviewing AMK's 11-year history, we do see times where the focus on data-driven decisions has faltered. For example, during the period of rapid growth (2007–09) a number of products were introduced as a result of Management decisions rather than rigorous research. One such instance of this was the launch of an urban loan product in 2010, which replicated AMK's rural methodology within an urban setting, without the prerequisite research on how the needs of urban poor people differed from those of rural clients. Another instance was the introduction in 2009 of a range of niche complementary non-financial services (such as solar lamps and water filters), and a special unit to deliver loans to vulnerable trafficked women. Despite their relevance to the needs of rural Cambodians, these services were introduced largely in response to external grant-funding opportunities rather than on a well-researched needs-based assessment. This departure from AMK's historically strong data-driven decision-making was highlighted in a due diligence conducted in early 2010 by Agora (a social investor intending to buy a majority stake in AMK from Concern at the time): 'AMK is regularly deciding what is good for clients instead of listening to them through its research'.

As a result, in the post-financial crisis consolidation phase, reliance on data and the need to understand clients (rather than making assumptions about them) was re-emphasized. The SPC also engaged increasingly in informing strategic planning and decision-making processes. In doing so, the committee's role has evolved. It serves to ensure the relevance of the Research department's work, giving feedback on its work plan, framing the research questions that underpin its work, and ensuring the rigour of research outputs. Perhaps more importantly, it helps the Board interpret research findings and understand their practical relevance. Through an innovative 'traffic light dashboard', it categorizes issues in terms of 'things are going well, so no implications'; 'urgent action needed'; or 'wait to see how this develops'. In all this, the SPC has a clear function in interrogating operational performance and research results, bringing in and using different perspectives to ask questions that might not occur to operational staff, and helping the organization better consider what it does and how it takes decisions.

. . . and between Research and Operations

In many organizations there is a serious disconnect between Research and Operations. When we think about the drivers of the reality gap between theory and practice, this is often one of the root causes: a research department that does research, and an operations department that implements, but little understanding and dialogue to link the two. Even when an organization has the right systems in place to support this, the link between Research and Operations should not be taken for granted, and is not always easy to manage. Operations has a momentum of its own, and staff who are in touch with clients every day often feel that they know their clients and what's best for them. Particularly when things seem to be going well, there's a tendency for staff to feel that more research is not relevant.

In AMK's early days, the connection between its Research department and the day-to-day issues that Operations was tackling was weak. If Operations identified an issue (such as a spike in repayment problems), operational staff did their own investigation, and any findings about what was working (or not) were not formally communicated between departments. However, over time AMK recognized the role of good conversations in linking good questions and good decisions. It was no longer a case of simply using research to produce a glossy report to land on the desk of the product design team leader. The Research department had strong skills in talking to clients, and in using its analytical ability to identify patterns and link these back to a deeper understanding of clients. However, if products and services were to be adjusted along the way, then Operations and Research would need to talk to each other constantly, through feedback and learning mechanisms that would provide timely and relevant insights enabling more market-responsive innovation. Over time, this connectedness between AMK's Operations and Research departments has strengthened, and the ability to segment and mine

AMK - SOCIAL PERFORMANCE REPORTING FRAMEWORK

	Regular monitoring				Periodic research
Period evaluated: 1 January to 31 December 2012					
Information presented 4 December 2012	Depth of outreach	Adequate products	Transparency & client protection	Other corporate social responsibility (CSR)	Change effects
Sources of information	– Depth of Outreach Report 2012 – Client Profile Report 2012	– Client Satisfaction Report 2012 – Exit Client Report 2012	– Microfinance Information Exchange (MIX), website, media kit (server) – Multiple Loans Report 2012 – Borrower awareness Client Grievance Report 2012	– Reasons for resignation of staff – Summary of Staff Satisfaction Report	– Change Report
Indicators	– Wellbeing score (tercile and quartile analysis) – Geographic targeting and client accessibility – Daily food expenditures vs. National Food Poverty Line (NFPL) – Household penetration by district – Pro-poor methodology (collateral, size, etc.)	– Range of services – Quality of services – Accessibility of services – Reasons for exiting – Rate of deserting	– Server access to information (within) – The MIX Market Updated – Profile of multiple loan holders by poverty group and repayment problems – Multiple loan rate found by Research department, Credit Bureau Check (CBC), and Internal Audit	– Staff turnover and explanations, especially turnover during probation – Human Resources policies	– Changes to clients' inflows and expenditures since 2006/2007 – Clients' asset holdings – Comparison of changes for clients with changes for non-clients

YEAR OF ASSESSMENT: 2008 (up to Sept) SOCIAL PERFORMANCE ASSESSMENT - SUMMARY

Methodology, process and reports/ Sources of information	Depth of outreach	Adequate products	Transparency & client protection	Other CSR	When applicable .... Change effects
Are you satisfied with the accuracy of the methodology and process applied?	Green	Green	Green	Green	Green
Is this result/finding in line with the mission?	Green	Green	Green	Green	Green
Based on these findings, are there foreseeable issues in the future?	Amber	Amber	Green	Green	Green
Is data or information appropriate / missing... ...at the Management level?	Green	Green	Green	Green	Green
...at the Board level?	Green	Green	Green	Green	Green
Issues to report	– In future include primary market savers (adapting methodology) – Review/update the Principal Component Analysis (PCA) model – New clients currently mirror poverty profile of comparison group (not an issue now, to keep an eye for next year(s))	– Data on savings/other multi-product clients – Revised methodology for both satisfaction and exit (focus group):	– Data on trends for client awareness – Data on trends for grievances – Data on client awareness and grievances should be analysed by Management at least twice a year	– To counteract resignation there is need for non-technical team building / in-house communication and especially for Management	– In future: Management / Board to decide upon key research priorities for AMK's widening product and customer base – Change study to be used as the base for an externally published article (putting findings into greater context)
Other issues — Other:					

Key: ■ Green light   ▌ Amber light

Figure 2.2 AMK's social performance dashboard

operational data has increased. Interestingly, having a more operational focus on research has led to a greater appreciation of the need to understand the *reasons* for client behaviour and experience, rather than just the patterns, with qualitative research now becoming a feature. As Pete Power (former AMK CEO) elucidates:

> An in-house, qualified and competent research function is incredibly useful. Most microfinance organizations don't have this capability, and so they contract external people. We can make decisions quite quickly as we have this capacity in-house; we can send researchers into the field overnight in response to a particular situation, event or trend. We have the databases and we can chart trends, etc. The data is all ours which means we can use it all the time, which we couldn't do if outsourced. Frankly, we mine the hell out of the data.

Using data better

To underline Pete Power's point, good conversations can only happen when data is available, and when it is being used well. AMK's information systems have evolved to strengthen its ability to move beyond product-design focused research, to research aimed at making adjustments and improvements based on more rigorous data analysis. In 2009, when cracks started appearing in AMK's operations in the wake of the global financial crisis, the Board flagged their concern that the information system was not providing timely portfolio data to Management. Information was held in a branch database that was periodically transferred manually to head office, meaning that Management only had consolidated data at the end of the month (and it was too time-consuming to look at all branches individually). The result was that follow-up on 'red flags' was slow or non-existent, and most managers were not looking at the data available to track staff and loan portfolio performance. Today, all branches are linked online through high-speed data connections, which gives head office Management access to real-time information – so red flags can be identified and followed up on the same day.

On the data analysis side, AMK developed its own management information platform, utilizing the Microsoft Analysis Services multidimensional reporting system (referred to as the 'Cube'), which allows data from the management information system (MIS) to be analysed in Microsoft Excel. This enables segmentation of client and performance data according to any of the variables captured, either for routine performance reporting or for on-demand data mining. Most importantly, it allows every manager complete flexibility to analyse data for their own area, branch, or region, or at an aggregate level, using variables of their own choosing to seek out patterns and trends. The Research department also uses the Cube to answer its own questions. For example, the head of the Research department, in looking at the reasons for client exit, noticed that a high number of clients were leaving because they were rejected by AMK. This led AMK to recognize that its policy on minimum group size was resulting in whole groups being rejected for repeat loans in cases where one person had left a group that was unable to recruit another member. As a result, AMK changed its policy to reduce the minimum group size from four to three.

Despite some initial resistance due to an unfamiliarity with quantitative data, the Cube technology is now well-liked by managers, and while it may not yet be used to its full potential in terms of exploring patterns and relationships, AMK as a whole is on a positive trajectory. To date, analysis has focused primarily on financial performance variables such as loan portfolio, repayment, and client exit according to, for example, type of client business, which is captured in the MIS. AMK recognizes the potential to improve this system in relation to data that is captured in the MIS and fed into the Cube. For example, poverty status is only captured for a sample of new clients (rather than for all clients), and much of the demographic data captured in the application form for new clients is not yet entered into the MIS. Neither does the system capture data such as client cash-flow generated during the loan appraisal, which could be used to track client performance.

AMK's desire for data-driven decision-making is linked to a recognition that a greater level of data about who the clients are, their experience of using AMK's products and services, and their outcomes, could improve AMK's ability to understand for whom its services are working well, and who might be struggling, all of which could feed into product and delivery improvements. The vision for this level of analysis certainly exists, although AMK needs to address the high cost and complexity of capturing this data from clients. A planned project to equip client officers with tablet computers will allow them to capture a much wider amount of client data, which would enable much more effective data analysis in the future, combining both portfolio and client analysis.

Another development in terms of information management is the impact of the recent diversification of financial products. AMK is becoming a multiproduct and multichannel organization (for example, the same savings products can be accessed through either a branch office or a village-based agent). This makes the information landscape more complex in terms of understanding clients and their needs, experiences, and behaviour – and the Research department and information analytical systems are evolving to meet these challenges.

Looking ahead

Good products (designed around facts, not assumptions) and good conversations (at every level) are an essential foundation of an organization designed to do good in the marketplace. That said, good organizations are about more than good products. The reality of delivering those products on the ground is quite complex, and practice often differs from theory in quite radical ways. AMK's experience highlights a lesson relevant to all social enterprises: that the model will fail if we let the social value in our products and services get lost in translation on the ground. This is our focus for Part II.

Notes

1. A *Prakas* (or government decree) on the 'Registration and Licensing of Micro-Finance Institutions' mandated that all non-governmental organization (NGO) microfinance operators with portfolios in excess of 1 billion Cambodian riel (at the time, approximately $254,000) transform into private companies (which, at the time, affected only six NGOs in the country, including the Concern programme).
2. Interesting reading on the role of rice in the Cambodian economy and diet can be found via World Food Programme here http://documents. wfp.org/stellent/groups/public/documents/ena/wfp099145.pdf
3. Solidarity lending is when small groups borrow collectively, and instead of putting up collateral against their loans, use mutual support to encourage each other to repay.
4. Technically speaking, snails do have blood, although owing to its chemical composition, it appears blue rather than red.

References

Chandararot, K. and Ballard, B. (2004) *Cambodia Annual Economic Review,* Phnom Penh: Cambodia Development Resource Institute.

Chetan, T. (2007) 'Are social and financial objectives mutually exclusive? The experience of AMK, Cambodia', *Small Enterprise Development* 18:1: 65–78, Rugby: Practical Action Publishing, <http://dx.doi.org/10.3362/0957-1329.2007.009>.

Di Certo, B. (2012) 'Flood-affected poor "drowning in debt"', *Phnom Penh Post* [online] <http://www.phnompenhpost.com/national/flood-affected-poor-%E2%80%98drowning-debt%E2%80%99> (23 February 2012) [accessed 26 August 2014].

Sinha, S. (2013) 'Microfinance in Cambodia: Investors' playground or force for financial inclusion?' [online paper] Gurgaon: M-CRIL, <www.m-cril.com/BackEnd/ModulesFiles/Publication/Cambodia_Analysis_1_2013.pdf> (December 2013) [accessed 26 August 2014]

PART II
Translating good intentions

In Part I of this book, we explored how social enterprises can move from good intentions and assumptions towards a well-researched and thoughtfully designed approach to delivering social value and avoiding harm. We also talked about the importance of asking good questions, and having good conversations, in ensuring that our work is as effective as possible. And yet still the best-laid plans don't always turn out as we envisioned. Too often in our work with organizations, we see a worrying reality gap emerge between theory and practice: between what an organization sets out to do (as enshrined in its strategy, products, and operational manuals), and what actually happens on the ground (in terms of how staff are working). Why is that? What is missing?

In answering this question, we're getting to the heart of what it means to make the essential leap from 'good products' to 'good organizations', and the starting point is to recognize that a key piece of the puzzle is … our people. Products and services are delivered by people; staff are managed by people; and organizations are governed by people. If we were to build the ideal social enterprise from the ground up, we would want to fill it with individuals who are motivated to keep a strong focus on doing good at the centre of everything that they do, so that its social value proposition is not 'lost in translation'.

Today, AMK is a business whose social mission is written into its very DNA. A walk through the organization, speaking to staff at random, reveals how many can accurately describe what AMK is trying to achieve and why, who the target clients are, and what their lives are like. On talking to Board members, it is clear they see the value of what AMK is trying to achieve as a social enterprise, and engage in ongoing dialogue about how to balance the social and commercial pressures of the institution's work. Most importantly, at every level, there is a sense of enthusiasm about both the significance and the success of AMK's work.

So was AMK just lucky to find the right people? It's a tempting conclusion to draw. Indeed, when we talked to Board members about various members of the AMK senior management team, a common refrain was: 'Oh, yes, they've made a really important contribution to the work of the organization. *We were lucky to find them.*' When you look at how AMK's roster of talent grew and developed over time, there's something in this statement that seems, at first glance, to ring true. From the management team, to the Research department, to the Board, different individuals seem to have brought the right skills the table at precisely the right time. Digging deeper into the organization as

http://dx.doi.org/10.3362/9781780448640.003

objective outsiders, however, we're inclined to reject this theory. It's not about luck – it's about having everyone in the organization working towards a clear and common goal.

But if it's not down to finding really switched-on staff, but rather making sure that everyone is committed to the organization's social value proposition, what is so difficult about that? Surely the mere fact of running (or being employed by) such a strongly mission-focused organization is ample motivation for keeping that mission in the frame? Not so, if we take the experience of the broader microfinance industry as our standard barometer. Managing the tension between an organization's social and commercial objectives is a delicate balancing act, and one that is susceptible to mis-calibration in the face of any number of internal or external influences. The dangers of getting this balance wrong can be seen in the ever-present spectres of mission drift and harmful outcomes for clients (such as over-indebtedness or harsh collection practices) – charges which have often been laid at the industry's door, particularly in recent years. While there's no doubt that microfinance was born of a genuine desire to benefit its clients, practitioners for too long assumed that positive outcomes were more or less automatic. Getting the products right is important – and AMK took a deliberate approach to thinking through what it wanted to do and how. More interesting than this, however, is that when it comes to achieving its social mission, AMK understood that it couldn't rely on mere altruism from staff. Its business model abounds with critical tension points (between doing good and doing well), which its people need to grapple with every day, especially when factoring in the pressure to grow and compete. And we're not just talking about the people at the top level (Management and Board); this applies equally to frontline staff, who are the most important interface between the institution and its clients.

For social enterprises, recognizing these tensions (and to whom they apply) is important. The first step in overcoming them is to ensure that we're not asking our people to choose between easy work and valuable work. The second step is to recognize that when it comes to product and service design, we don't always get it right first time. When it comes to improving the work that we do, we should be innovating from the ground up.

Managing what matters

All businesses must manage the quality and consistency of their product and service delivery in order to succeed in the marketplace: delivering value isn't just about good design, it's also about the detail of how it is delivered. For social purpose organizations, too often the details that are important from a social value perspective (such as spending the time necessary to understand the risks that a client faces) are not recognized in management systems. Where value for clients is assumed (or not fully understood), the danger is that quality will be managed according to commercial measures alone (for example, by focusing purely on the number of loans given and whether they are repaid on time, rather than considering the reasons why clients are failing to repay).

Put our people into a challenging environment with high productivity targets, and this task becomes all the more difficult. In a social enterprise, Management might understand that there may be 'win-win' outcomes in terms of serving clients well, but staff might have a different take on the situation. Travelling for hours on a pot-holed dirt road may help the organization reach its mission of serving poor people in far-flung corners of the country, and may even be worthwhile in terms of developing new markets, but it will feel like difficult work for staff, who may feel they are driving past (seemingly) hundreds of potential clients in less remote areas along the way. And when we ask staff to reach more people with smaller loans (rather than offering larger loans to fewer, better-off people), in practice they are being asked to do more work, and where this means more travel, potentially more difficult work. When we build in aspects of the organization's methodology (such as loan appraisals, in the case of microfinance) that are designed to protect clients from harm, we need to be aware that these require staff to spend more time with each client. In the face of high productivity targets, staff might be tempted to cut corners on these critical elements in order to serve more clients.

If we're looking to do good, and do well, within the marketplace, the devil is in the detail. The core of the work lies not just in the big picture of doing good, but in the precise detail of what needs to be delivered to whom and in what way. As social enterprises, it's also important to clearly identify the crunch points between our social and financial imperatives, and the points at which we are at the most risk of failing to do good, or doing harm. Once we can do this, we're equipped to ensure that our staff understand these tensions, are trained to approach them effectively, and are incentivized and managed to deliver what is expected.

Don't forget the governance

It's not just frontline staff who are susceptible to the tensions between the social and commercial priorities inherent in the business model. It is at Board level where an organization grapples with the 'big think', strategic business model issues that resonate throughout its operations. Unless Board decisions are driven by an adequate understanding of client needs, and the processes that are important to achieving social value (the devilish detail), they run the risk of pulling levers that will lead to unintended consequences. For example, by bowing to either pressure or opportunity within the marketplace, many organizations have embarked on growth at a pace too rapid to uphold quality, or have set performance targets that can only be met if staff cut corners with their target clients, or indeed focus on non-target clients. What we find interesting about AMK's experience is that it took a deliberate approach to involve its governance in tackling these tensions. It made sure the right people were sitting at the table; that they were clear about the AMK's social value proposition; that they were trained and motivated to manage tensions arising in the business model; and that they had the information needed to do so successfully. As we highlighted in Chapter 2, ensuring that the Board has good conversations, and enabling it to use this information well, has been key to making this work.

The end of 'command and control'

Managing quality is important because it's far from automatic, and opportunities to let this focus slip abound in the context of difficult work. That said, when organizations find that things aren't happening on the ground quite as planned, it's not always due to a lack of clarity and good management. In fact, sometimes, when theory differs from practice, it can be a very good thing.

Sounds like quite a radical idea. Or perhaps not, if we look at it through our 'social value lens'. It might be nice to think that organizations can be run by pulling levers from the centre, and that clients' lives can be changed in predictable and formulaic ways, but the world is not as ordered and predictable as we might like. In addition to the 'hard' side of building organizational processes and systems to deliver value, there is a critical 'soft' side to organizational culture: how staff engage with the purpose of the organization, reflect on what they are doing, and contribute to learning and improving practice.

Having your staff on your side by ensuring they understand what you are trying to do, focus on delivering your intent (and not just following the letter of their job description), and continue to learn and improve, is key to being effective. AMK learned that, in cases where the reality on the ground differed from the theory in its training and manuals, this needed to be communicated to Management with a view to leading to improved practice. Building an organizational culture to make this happen has been a key part of AMK's success, and we'll explore this more in Chapters 3 and 4.

CHAPTER 3

Insight: Do what it says on the tin

To be honest, when I was promoted to manager of one of the branches in arrears in 2010, I saw that the problems were so bad, I wasn't sure I would be able to fix them. The cause of the problems was clear enough: Management had lost control of quality at branch level – and Operations was happy with our rate of growth. But no one was stopping to ask why we were growing so fast, and whether this was a good thing or a bad thing.

Along the way, however, staff started making serious mistakes. Some staff weren't collecting the right information from clients – one client officer didn't even talk to a client directly, but talked to the client's aunt, who was the village bank president, assuming that she would give reliable information. What the aunt was doing was putting her nephew into debt on his behalf. In such cases, how can the client officer be sure it's not too much debt? In other instances, staff weren't checking the information that clients provided. For example, an individual loan client gave some information about their cash-flow, based on the price of rice in the market. The client officer didn't know the price of rice – so he just wrote down whatever the client said without checking it with someone more knowledgeable about such things. It turns out the client was wrong – and in the case of that client using their future income to estimate repayment capacity for an individual loan, that's a real problem. I also found instances where client officers let many members of the same family take out a loan, or accepted clients with loans from other organizations, even though we had policies against this. Some client officers were submitting up to 60 new loan applications a day – which is impossible if you're doing all the proper checks – but the former Branch Manager didn't complain. All the incentives at that time were focused on getting more and more clients, so it was 'short-term growth, hello; long-term quality, bye-bye.' We had a lot of warning signs I guess, but either the information wasn't getting through on time, or it was just being ignored. So was it any wonder that bad debt had reached 5 per cent?

I decided to start by turning around staff culture. There was a bad culture at the time – staff weren't committed to clients, and they were quite negative about AMK after the previous Branch Manager was fired for fraud. I knew that I needed to understand their hearts, and help them find motivation for doing a good job again. So I went out into the villages, I took client officers into areas they thought they couldn't penetrate, and showed them how to do it. I did a lot of training and coaching of field staff – and rebuilt the team from the ground up. We focused on working with clients who had bad debts – looking at whether or not they were willing, and whether or not they were able to repay. We started with those with the willingness and the ability to repay. We re-analysed their cash-flow, and negotiated a new repayment plan based on that. We didn't pressure clients to repay, but we did make it clear they were responsible – and followed up with every one of them twice a month by phone or a visit. Two years later, when I was promoted to regional manager, my branch was the third best branch in AMK, and many of my staff were promoted as well.

AMK Branch Manager

This Branch Manager's story describes an unexpected twist in AMK's tale. As an organization, it had put a lot of time and effort into understanding the reality of its clients' lives, and using this to drive its product design. It had also applied this social value lens to its ongoing conversations around what was working, for whom, and what it could be doing better. In terms of a 'model organization' built to deliver social value within the marketplace – so far, so good. Yet the story above highlights that AMK came to a point in its history where cracks started to show in its operations: staff weren't doing what they needed to do; clients were potentially being put at risk; and Management wasn't acting on the warning signs. So what went wrong?

The bottom line is this: working at AMK is the opposite of an easy, comfortable desk job; it is a physically and intellectually demanding way of making a living. While all this effort delivers payoffs in the end for lender and clients alike, the level of effort required to make it all work correctly carries with it the temptation for staff save time by cutting corners. This could slip beneath the attention of managers who are not focused on the right things.

The question this raises for all social enterprises is: how can we 'do what it says on the tin', and succeed in doing what we claim to do? If good intentions are not enough, and informed product design and improvement aren't enough, then what is? Exploring the middle years of AMK's history, when things started to go wrong and its business model experienced a significant stress test, provides some key insights into what it means to move from an organization with good intentions to an organization that is doing good.

Laying the foundation for growth

Let's begin by setting the scene. From its inception, AMK had a grand vision for what it could achieve. At the first Board meeting of 2003, AMK set its compass towards becoming a leader in microfinance in Cambodia. The Framework Agreement with Concern (see Introduction) guaranteed funding until 2005, which meant that AMK had two years to complete the transformation and commercialization process and achieve financial self-sufficiency. As it did so, it focused on putting in place the 'nuts and bolts' of an efficient, effective, and well-run organization that could reach scale. Outreach to cover large numbers of poor people throughout the country was central, and so too was the need to base success on serving the needs of clients in a transparent and cost-effective way.

Streamlining operations

AMK inherited from Concern a strongly mission-driven staff, but a portfolio haemorrhaging funds. For this reason, early Board minutes reflect a strong concern with putting in place the building blocks for a successful business. Many who were part of AMK at the time describe the organization then as a 'start-up'. Although its operations on the ground were sizeable, there was very little capacity in head office (as the branches had previously been managed through the Concern country office), and its systems and structures were those of a charity programme rather than a financial institution. For example, when AMK set up its own finance department, separate from the project accounting of Concern, it took three whole months for Management to get a clear picture of the real state of the organization's finances. Policies, procedures and operations manuals had to be developed; staff trained; financial systems established. In the field, substantial 'clean-up' was needed to identify all loan clients and follow up with large numbers of non-paying clients.[1]

Another focus was to remove some of the inefficiencies inherited from Concern and reduce the very high operating costs. These inefficiencies were manifest in the methodology, and also institutional processes. For example, AMK undertook a complete organizational overhaul by reviewing (and in many cases creating new) policies, procedures, and systems. Many of the policies in place at the time made the loan application process time-consuming for both staff and clients. These were reviewed and, where it was clear that they were not essential in delivering value, avoiding harm for clients, or reducing risk for AMK, they were discarded or modified. Changes included removing certain requirements: to have a photograph of clients, an endorsement signature by the chief (often requiring informal payment by clients), a one-month gap between completion of a loan and renewal, and compulsory attendance at group meetings. Decision-making was decentralized, giving Branch Managers, for example, the ability to handle branch bank accounts and sign cheques for loan disbursement; previously they would have had to send a request to the head office – a highly inefficient process involving a week's delay in disbursement, in addition to the cost of transport as cheques were returned by car. Devolving responsibility also led to improved performance, as regional and branch staff became more focused, empowered, and energized.

Strengthening management systems . . .

To ensure that staff were reaching the right clients and working with them in the right way, AMK also developed its management systems and incentives. Given its efforts to calibrate its social and commercial aims, staff incentives needed to reflect this balance, driving those aspects of delivery that were important to creating social value for clients while recognizing AMK's small profit margins and consequent need for productivity. Where productivity is pushed too far, the quality of service delivery starts to slip. Where portfolio at risk is pushed too far, there's a danger that staff will put too much pressure on clients to repay. And where portfolio size is pushed too far, the risk is that staff pressure clients to accept higher loans than they can afford, or give bigger loans to fewer (better-off) clients.

The staff incentive scheme provides monthly, performance-based, financial bonuses up to a maximum 35 per cent of basic salary for client officers (although few achieve this level of performance); it also rewards managers and head office staff for achieving performance benchmarks. In the early years the incentives sought to balance outreach to clients (number of clients) with the amount of money lent and the recovery rate (a signal that clients are able to repay their loans). In this way, simply giving out more money to more clients would not earn the bonus – the client officer had to focus both on reaching a large number of clients, and on ensuring that clients received the right loan for their capacity, thus ensuring high rates of repayment.

But AMK not only incentivized staff to focus on providing the right loans to clients; it sought to motivate them to go the extra mile to serve poor, rural clients. As we shall discuss in Chapter 5, AMK actively sought to expand in the more remote, rural areas of the country. In this way, 'going the extra mile' was wholly literal: client officers often needed to travel 200–300 km on a daily basis by motorbike, often negotiating treacherous terrain such as mountain passes, poor-quality dirt roads, and rivers prone to flooding. Recognizing the challenges associated with the job, AMK's performance evaluation system also includes adjustments for the 'potential' of the area where a client officer works, and does not create negative incentives to work in areas that are more difficult than others.

. . . and relationships

Beyond these incentives was a recognition that a transparent and respectful relationship between staff and clients was critical – and AMK put a lot of effort into getting this relationship right. To avoid staff putting clients under too much pressure to repay their loans, and strengthen other aspects of the staff-client relationship, in 2005 AMK established a code of practice for client protection (see Box: 'AMK's code of practice for client protection'). This set out its commitment to sell the right products, in the right way, to its clients, giving them the information they needed to make good decisions upfront, and helping them when things went wrong. That AMK developed its code of practice three years before global efforts started to define the meaning of client protection in microfinance, is remarkable. To ensure it was delivering on this intention, AMK integrated the code into its operating policies and procedures, and monitoring systems.

The effort that AMK put into establishing these basic business building blocks (developing its systems, streamlining the methodology, and putting

---

AMK's code of practice for client protection

Inclusion: AMK will maximize the inclusion of the poor and other marginalized populations with AMK's products and services.

Avoidance of over-indebtedness: AMK will limit client exposure to their capacity to repay and will seek to avoid client over-indebtedness.

Transparent pricing: AMK will provide its clients with complete information on its product features, costs, and obligations, and will ensure transparency in all product and transaction pricing.

Ethical staff behaviour: AMK will ensure ethical and respectful behaviour of staff towards clients.

Freedom of choice: AMK will facilitate and promote freedom of choice to its clients.

Appropriate collection practices: AMK's debt collection practices will be reasonable and collaborative, and never abusive or coercive.

Mechanisms for redress of grievances: AMK will provide clients with appropriate and accessible mechanisms for complaint and problem resolution.

Privacy of client data: The privacy of client data will be respected unless disclosure is required by law.

---

quality checks into place) paid real dividends. By the end of 2005, AMK had increased its staff numbers by 50 per cent, and doubled its client and village outreach. The foundations for a healthy organization, which could effectively serve large numbers of poor people, were in place.

Stress testing the model

At the same time as AMK was poised for significant organizational growth, so too was the Cambodian economy as a whole, driven by the tourism, garment and construction industries. Between 2004 and 2008, GDP growth (exceeding 10 per cent per annum) allowed AMK clients to take advantage of abundant opportunities, and to be reasonably certain that they would have the funds to repay a loan. Between 2005 and 2009, AMK expanded rapidly, growing from just 3 branches to 22 branches and 50 sub-branches, and prioritized the poorest provinces and villages in its outreach efforts. This growth mirrored that of the sector as a whole, with Cambodia being one of the fastest growing microfinance markets in the world at that time (Sinha, 2013). In terms of staff workload, productivity levels soared from 539 borrowers per client officer in 2004, to 937 at the end of 2006. Given its focus on rural outreach, this meant that AMK was asking its staff to do incredibly demanding work.

On arrival at a village bank meeting, after physically difficult travel between villages, client officers need to conduct their business respectfully, accurately and efficiently. When challenges arise for clients, field staff need to come up with effective solutions on the spot and, when their caseload increased, staff had a lot of potential problems to solve. Field staff also need to invest time in ensuring that groups are well formed and trained; that village bank presidents are trained and supervised to assist with much of the monitoring and trouble-shooting; and that one-on-one loan appraisals are conducted with care. Each discrete task is critical to the smooth running of the loan process, and enhances clients' chances of success.

Staff growth also played a lead role in this narrative. Outreach to more and more clients meant taking on new staff to serve those clients, and other new staff to train, support, and manage those frontline staff. As AMK's client outreach grew in the six years up to 2009, its staff roster swelled eleven-fold. Perhaps the dynamics of a small, close-knit team would have generated sufficient motivation to stay mission-focused. Within the context of rapid growth, however, AMK was under pressure to maintain clarity, and ensure that the message about what the organization was trying to achieve, and why, was not lost in translation, as more and more staff joined, began working at a greater distance from the head office, and operating within a hierarchy of Area Managers and Branch Managers.

But the pressure to cut corners didn't just stem from the fact that AMK aims to do difficult work. It also arose because the competition seemingly *doesn't*. When you drive down the main street in a Cambodian town – even many of the smaller ones – the first thing you might notice is the sheer number of financial service providers operating there. The second thing you might notice is just how *nice* their offices are. The accomplishment of AMK's competition is firmly visible in these colourful, sleek, modern, glass-fronted palaces rising high into the sky. Standing out amid the sea of modest, makeshift (often ramshackle) enterprises surrounding them, they ooze financial success and trustworthiness; an important message for a population fearful of losing their life savings to banks that might very well lock their doors and close down (as others have in the past). Having set the scene, consider it from the perspective of AMK staff, going to work every day in the institution's relatively humble branches. Not only did high levels of market competition put pressure on AMK to succeed in commercial terms, but the competition stayed in easier-to-reach areas *and* had much nicer offices.

Losing quality

As we discussed in Part I, AMK put a lot of time and effort into understanding its clients' needs and designing appropriate products to create value and avoid harm. In doing so, it built a number of 'valuable' elements into its methodology that were critical for supporting and protecting clients. However it is clear that these elements, designed to ensure quality delivery, started to slip in practice. The Branch Manager's story that we just heard offers a window into cracks in the loan appraisal process, which was core to ensuring that clients did not take on more debt than they could afford.

For group clients, a visit to the client's home has historically been a keystone of this process, occurring before the loan is approved and disbursed. It consists of a 15–20-minute interview in the client's home, during which time the client officer runs through a set of questions to get a sense of the client's living conditions and income-generating capacity. The visit helps to establish or maintain the relationship between field staff and clients but, more importantly, it is a key opportunity for the former to assess whether the latter can handle the level of debt they have requested, and whether it will be invested wisely.

If you think this sounds like a good idea from a client protection perspective, you'd be right. The benefits for the institution (in terms of not approving a loan that cannot be repaid) and the client (in terms of avoiding the perils of excess debt) are clear – and fully in line with AMK's guiding principles. However, this aspect of the methodology also involves real trade-offs for everyone concerned. From a client perspective, it means a longer interval between requesting and actually receiving a loan (up to two weeks for a new village bank), which, given increased competition and the wide choice of financial service providers, could make a loan from a different microfinance organization seem more attractive. For AMK, however, this more cautious, cash-flow based approach to lending is critical to avoiding harm – meaning that (in the words of one senior manager), AMK will 'never be the leader in customer service, as it is conventionally defined'. From an institutional perspective, the home visit represents a significant drag on AMK's productivity, adding an estimated one day per month to the average client officer's workload.

So, the home visit is a costly and (from the client's point of view) potentially unappealing addition to the lending process; and Management and staff haven't always understood clearly just how valuable this process is in terms of protecting clients. For an institution operating in difficult areas and with slim profit margins, efficiency was key – and increasing caseloads resulted in a decreased emphasis on the home visit. It was still a primary aspect of the product design, and was written into the lending manual for staff. However, under pressure from AMK's growth, financial considerations became much more salient for client officers. For this reason, it became accepted practice to complete the loan appraisal process during the village bank meeting, rather than in the home where client officers could get a real sense of how the client lived and worked. Worse still, in some instances appraisals were being conducted for 5–10 clients at a time, meaning that individual clients weren't getting the attention they needed, and were missing out on an opportunity to establish a supportive relationship with the client officer. Lacking a real understanding of the importance of the home visit, Management wasn't checking to see whether it was happening, focusing energy instead on the volume of loans disbursed and repaid.

Risky practice

But perhaps the biggest concern over quality delivery involved AMK's indi-vidual loan product. Comparing the 2007 and 2008 year-end results, we see a remarkable change in the profile of who AMK is reaching. The percentage of individual (rather than group) loan clients jumps from 6 to 15 per cent. So, while overall year-to-year client growth is relatively consistent, in 2008 *nearly one third* of new clients took individual loans – as opposed to *less than 8 per cent* of new clients the year before. When we look at the percentage of total money lent, this trend becomes even more dramatic: individual loans nearly double, growing from 20 to 35 per cent of the portfolio in this one year.

So what was going on here? And was this it actually a problem? To understand the significance of this shift and the risk it created for AMK, it's useful to revisit the thinking behind the introduction of the individual loan product in the first place. As described in Chapter 1, the individual loan was geared towards clients with regular income streams, who could pay back in regular monthly instalments (rather than at the end of the loan term, as with the majority of AMK's group loan products). It was also designed for clients with relatively big economic baskets, who needed larger loans to take advantage of business opportunities. As such, whereas group loan caps were the equivalent of US$50 for the first loan, and $125 for subsequent cycles, the individual loan gave clients access to a first-cycle equivalent of $250, and $500 thereafter. AMK put in place strict loan appraisals, collateral requirements, and a monthly instalment feature, to protect it from the risk of lending these larger amounts. In addition, tight supervision (each loan request needed to be approved by both the Area Manager and Branch Manager) meant that there was a natural limit on how much these loans could grow.

In 2007, in response to a strong demand for individual loans (and therefore a market opportunity to grow), a number of changes were made that led to a dramatic uptake of these loans: the addition of a four-month grace period, and the extension of the repayment period from 12 to 18 months, served to make the instalments more manageable to clients and increase demand. In addition, whereas individual loans had previously been viewed with caution, client officers themselves were now allowed to recruit individual clients. The requirement for Branch Manager approval was also removed. This policy relaxation, however, was not accompanied by a tightening of the incentive scheme, which calculated bonuses in relation to each client officer's total portfolio (recall that individual loans were several times larger than group loans). While this might have been tempered by the incentive system requirement to reach a large number of clients, the incentive became distorted, because one individual loan counted as three group loans in the client number calculation. Given all this, it is easy to see how it suddenly became much more attractive for client officers to shift their focus to individual rather than group clients, and there was a rapid rise in individual loans.

Linked to this was the fact that the processes in place to deal with individual loans were inadequate. Client officers had been trained to complete group loan appraisals effectively, but the individual loan cash-flow appraisal process was more complex; without adequate training, the quality of the process suffered. This resulted in many clients without regular income streams graduating from the end-of-term group loan product to the larger individual loan product, even when the terms of the latter didn't necessarily line up with their cash-flow.

Beware of complacency

It is important to state upfront that AMK's story is not one of reckless growth followed by collapse; the 'Icarus Paradox'[2] of business school teaching highlights how, often, at the time of seemingly greatest success, the seeds of failure are being sown. During AMK's period of rapid growth there had been an awareness of the risks involved, particularly in terms of demands on Management and potential loss of quality. Indeed, the 2007 strategic plan emphasized growth with quality, stating:

> AMK recognizes that growth is a function of a number of variables, especially the quality and suitability of products/services and competition amongst providers. Its strategy is not so much driven by achievement of growth as by ensuring optimum quality and designing appropriate products. It beieves that growth is a by-product of these aspects and therefore need not be pursued vigorously as an objective by itself.

That said, the success in financial performance and growth did create a sense of complacency at both Management and Board level: 'The fact that we were exceeding every target ... it kind of blinds you a little bit' (former (CEO) Pete Power). One senior Operations Manager even went so far as to tell the Chief Operations Officer that: 'Portfolio at risk will never go above 1 per cent', only a few months before AMK felt the impact of the financial crisis. We talked to one Branch Manager who recalled criticism from a peer for his comparatively poor branch portfolio growth. He wasn't pushing bigger loans, but rather making sure his staff did good loan assessment based on clients' businesses – which meant that his branch was falling behind others in terms of growth. He also recalled the moment that other branches started experiencing repayment problems (while his branch did not), and how the criticism stopped then and there.

Systems for maintaining quality did weaken and, in the context of pressure to grow, shortcuts were taken, and in some places poor practice went unnoticed or unremarked. Importantly, internal control did not keep up with the growth of the organization, and was unable to provide adequate information to Senior Management about these losses in quality. Board minutes in 2007 report that the inspections department was not able to keep pace with its audit schedule, and Branch Managers were 'too busy' to do proper checks and reconciliations. By the end of 2007, the Board was urging Management to take steps to ensure that growth did not come at the expense of effective internal control. However, changes at Board level in 2008 meant that, often, issues of concern raised at one meeting were not followed up at the next, when different people were sat around the table.

The wake-up call – and a slow Board reaction

While the immediate impacts of these losses of quality were not dramatic, the growth of this inadequately managed product created significant risk for the organization and clients alike. AMK was no longer effectively managing what mattered. The financial crisis hit, exposing cracks in the system. This provided an important 'wake-up call' for the organization, prompting a renewed focus not just on what the organization was trying to do, but how it was trying to do it.

By 2009, the country was feeling the confluence of three debilitating shocks: high food and fuel cost inflation; the global financial crisis (felt in Cambodia mostly in late 2008 and 2009); and subsequent flooding on a national scale. Combined, these had a particularly damaging effect on the very sectors that had become the drivers of growth in the Cambodian economy – as evidenced by a rapid plunge in GDP growth from 10 per cent in 2010 to just 0.1 per cent in 2009. In the garment sector, for example, more than 70 factories closed, taking more than 70,000 jobs out of the economy, as highlighted in a 2011 study by the International Labour Organization (ILO).

Suddenly, the income sources that clients relied on to repay their loans dried up. While rural group clients with small loans mostly coped, AMK saw a significant increase in clients with individual loans struggling to repay them. Many of these had been granted without effective appraisal to match the loan to the client's cash-flow, and individual clients lacked the supportive group mechanism designed to help them solve repayment problems. Moreover, the rush for growth in the microfinance sector had also exposed clients in some areas to the opportunity to borrow from multiple sources. In line with its focus on client protection, AMK had a strict policy against lending to clients with an outstanding loan from another microfinance organization; this may have reduced the incidence of multiple borrowing, although of course it did not stop clients borrowing elsewhere after they had done so from AMK.

High levels of debt, combined with a loss of client income, resulted in a spike in clients defaulting on their loan, indicated by a sharp rise in bad debt for the individual loan product. Many clients found themselves with loans they simply could not repay. The response of most microfinance organizations in the sector at the time was to enforce collateral recovery, leading in numerous cases to confiscation of land and houses (the most common forms of guarantee). AMK's 'soft collections' approach to clients in crisis, which required Board approval to seize collateral, stood in stark contrast, focusing instead on understanding and solving problems with those clients who had a genuine willingness to repay, but not the capacity.

During these years, AMK felt the impact of the financial crisis in terms of increased bad debt. However, given the slim margins of AMK's business model, its profitability drop was significantly greater than that of its competitors. The fact that a bad debt level of 2.85 per cent – a normal level in many parts of the world – could almost wipe out AMK's profits, highlights the vulnerability of the organization at that time.

Despite these warning signs, Management and the Board were slow to react; one senior manager describes the organization as operating on 'autopilot'. By January 2009, bad debt had increased five-fold during one quarter, from 0.07 per cent to 0.36 per cent; Board minutes reported the increase, but concluded that portfolio quality was still high. By April 2009 bad debt was up to 1.57 per cent and the problem had been acknowledged; but as late as August 2009, with portfolio at risk at 2.3 per cent, the Board minutes described this as 'favourable compared to market trends', and the CEO reported to the Board that there was 'a clear focus on portfolio quality which was being strongly emphasized at every level within the organization'. Bad debt was highlighted as being concentrated in particular parts of the country, and in the individual loan product. While there was clearly concern at Board level, and a refusal to simply chalk up these problems to the global financial crisis, the Board did not ask clear questions about what was happening and what Management were doing to fix it – and therefore lacked clear answers from Management.

Learning the lessons

Overall, the ripple effects from the financial crisis gave the organization a hard knock and had a big impact on both Operations and head office staff, who experienced an increased workload in fixing the problems while receiving no performance bonuses for two years. At the same time, like all Cambodians, AMK staff saw their own standard of living fall owing to inflationary price increases. All that said, this period was also a time of learning, which helped the organization re-focus and strengthen. Operations staff interviewed were very clear that AMK is a much stronger organization now than it was in 2010: 'We learnt a lot from the crisis. We have experience of dealing with client issues, our processes are much stronger, and we have spread risk exposure by increasing the number of products we offer.'

The story of AMK's missteps, and subsequent corrections, provide a compelling insight: even the most immaculately designed product can fail once it has been launched – and this is true for organizations across the profit spectrum. Simply put, quality delivery is essential, and it is by no means the automatic outcome of good design. For social enterprises, brilliant concepts can go horribly awry when there's a lack of clarity at the staff and management level about the core drivers of social value for a given product; and these often come down to the detail around how that product is delivered. AMK's experience highlights that for microfinance organizations (especially in a competitive marketplace), great design can also fall foul of institutional pressure to grow. Socially valuable aspects of the lending methodology can be lost (deliberately, or through oversight) in the name of productivity, as staff take on increasing numbers of clients and feel pressure to streamline the service relationship, and as management prioritizes business aspects over social aspects.

For AMK, whose customer relationship extends beyond a simple 'buyer beware', ensuring that clients succeed means delivering the right products, in the right way. In early 2010, Agora (the social investor that was poised to buy the majority of Concern's shares in the company) carried out a due diligence visit. This highlighted significant weaknesses in AMK's culture, management and systems. As a result of this, and the post-financial crisis wake-up call, AMK has strengthened its processes to ensure that what matters (for both the client and for AMK) is adequately monitored and managed.

What does this mean in practice? Simply put, it is about making sure that operational staff know which aspects of delivery are critical to ensuring that the business relationship creates the desired social value, doesn't put clients at risk of harm, and delivers on organizational targets. Once AMK had identified what was important, it integrated those aspects into the way that it trained and incentivized its staff, and into the way that it carried out spot-checks for quality through the internal auditing process. Asking staff to do difficult work is not problematic in itself, but when the tensions between social and financial imperatives put pressure on those elements of our work that are designed to ensure quality, then we need to counter them with strong systems to make sure quality is upheld.

Why is all of this essential? There are a number of reasons. Firstly, by ensuring that field staff clearly understand what is operationally important, the institution empowers them to make effective decisions about how they use their time, and to maintain the core drivers of value when there's pressure on that time. Secondly, inasmuch as manager spot-checks and internal audits are designed to verify compliance with an organization's objectives, they are also used to keep tabs on issues around quality delivery. As managers and auditors generally have limited time to conduct their checks, the critical question is, what aspects of service delivery will be covered? The old adage 'what gets valued gets measured, and what gets measured gets managed' applies here. If AMK had indeed been on autopilot during its period of fast growth, then suddenly, it reverted to manual control.

The first thing to fix was the individual loan product, which was at the heart of AMK's loss of performance. This was pulled off the market with immediate effect, and later redesigned and cautiously reintroduced (as we'll learn in Chapter 5).

The next priority was to improve the systems for quality management. To address the problem of staff taking shortcuts and overlooking crucial steps in the methodology, AMK reformed its policies and procedures and supervision processes. By overlaying a social value lens on its internal audit function, AMK now gets regular insights into whether the critical touch-points with clients (identified at the design stage, and encouraged at the delivery stage) are actually happening (and whether they are happening well). For example, we see a renewed focus on home visits as part of the group loan appraisal. Management estimates that by 2009, this supposedly mandatory aspect of the methodology was actually taking place in only two-thirds of new loan applications. As a result, AMK instituted a zero tolerance policy for staff who skipped them, and integrated checks on home visits into the regular branch visits undertaken by the internal audit department. This led, in 2010, to a series of tough decisions to terminate the employment of client officers who had ignored the home visit requirement. However once these stories had circulated through the organization, compliance improved and the issue was effectively resolved.

AMK also took another look at its incentives. Today, AMK's incentive system looks at portfolio quality, portfolio size *and* client outreach (especially when it comes to individual lending). To ensure that clients aren't taking on excess debt, good loan appraisal is also considered. The number of clients is weighted more heavily than total portfolio size, and importantly, the weighting still takes into account the added difficulty of working in harder-to-reach areas (to avoid negatively incentivizing reaching poorer and more remote clients).

At an organizational level, there was a sense that head office costs had become too high – partly because of the non-financial projects. These were terminated, and measures introduced to improve efficiency.

Looking ahead

The importance of managing what matters is a valuable lesson for any social enterprise. While it is true that AMK learned this lesson the hard way, it is also true that the corrective actions that it took as a result have made it into a stronger, more resilient organization, focused on its core principles. In this respect, the global financial crisis came at just the right time for AMK. But when we talk about the importance of an organization that learns from its experience, this doesn't just apply to the people at the top. Learning from mistakes, and learning from clients, happens at every level of an organization – and perhaps most critically on the frontlines. In Chapter 4, we will examine how AMK built a culture of learning from the outset, and how this culture of reflection and conversation was strengthened after the global financial crisis wake-up call.

CHAPTER 4
Insight: Motivate staff to do difficult work in an excellent way

Dark clouds were a bad sign. As I left the branch that morning, I thought of the day ahead – three hours of travel up through the mountains before two village bank meetings, and another three hours of travel back home. Would I make it back in time before the heavy rains started? I hoped so – I had come to enjoy visiting these remote villages, they reminded me of my own when I was a little boy, and the clients always greeted me warmly. An hour after I set off, the clouds opened. I was used to travelling in the rain, but what really worried me was what I saw when I reached the river halfway there. These were the mango-washing rains, signalling the end of the long dry season. By then, the ground was baked so hard that the rains didn't penetrate it. The waters of the river were rising fast – fed by all the water coming down from the hills. I knew that it would likely be flooded by evening, and I wouldn't be able to return. Should I turn back now? I could have easily called my Branch Manager and told her that I didn't want to risk getting stranded for a night. But then I thought about what the rains really meant – not for me, but for my clients. I was going to disburse their new loans, money that they would use to buy fertilizer for their rice paddies. Timing is everything. If I didn't get the money to them today, I wouldn't have time to return for a few more weeks – but by then it would be too late to get their paddies ready for planting, and they might have a bad season as a result. I didn't want to let them down. So I crossed the bridge, knowing that by evening it might not be there to see me safely back across. The clients were glad to see me, and of course glad to see the rains. As I suspected, the bridge was under water by the time I reached it. So I found a sheltered place in the forest and slept the night there – wet, uncomfortable, and quite hungry by morning, but most of all happy that I made the right decision.

Som Vuthy, Phreah Bihea Branch client officer

Vuthy's story raises an interesting question: when we say that our staff 'go the extra mile', what do we really mean? Of course, it's relatively straightforward to talk about 'miles' in the literal sense of the word. In the case of AMK, the organization was asking its staff to do very difficult work: long hours of travel through challenging terrain. In Vuthy's case, the extra mile was sleeping rough in a forest for the night; forsaking not only comfort, but his physical safety: putting himself at the mercy of tigers, snakes, wild boars and a whole host of other equally unsavoury animals.

Yet what strikes us most about this story is that Vuthy went the extra mile in a metaphorical sense: he saw that what he needed to do would be difficult, but he understood why it was important, and he was sufficiently motivated to do it anyway. In fact, such stories abound in the offices of AMK. When we talked to field staff, tales relating to difficult terrain, long distances travelled, motorbike breakdowns, and swollen rivers were common. However, the significance of these stories is not that AMK is a terrible place to work. Rather, staff wear them as a badge of pride: 'We like our work. It's difficult, but we know why it's important, and we believe in it.'

This raises a key point in terms of exploring what it means to build an organization for good. Quality products are important, and in the context of putting your people into difficult situations, so too is the recognition that quality delivery is far from automatic. When AMK saw that theory and practice weren't lining up, it strengthened the hard systems by which it managed the quality of its people's work: namely its policies, audits and incentives. Such hard systems, however, rely on the world being ordered and predictable. In the case of AMK, they set out a narrow 'order of operations' for client officers to follow in their work, one step following another, so that at the end of the process, the client benefits. The reality, however, is often a lot messier – especially when it comes to the lives of poor and vulnerable people. In those instances where practice actually needs to differ from theory, a command and control from the centre approach can fall short. Why? Because, in the context of unpredictable influences, the best product design or delivery system can sometimes be made better. Changing lives is not routine, uncreative work, and sometimes it means coming up with more effective solutions to a problem.

Against this background, AMK understands that that when it comes to people doing difficult, excellent work (and doing it better all the time), the 'soft stuff' matters too. Hard systems are good at framing what staff need to do – but do they help staff fully appreciate *why it is important*? In the case of AMK, client officers might be trained and managed to appraise new loan applications effectively, but do they understand the impact that the correct loan size will have on the client's investment and ability to repay? And just because staff understand why something is important, doesn't mean they will automatically be motivated to do it (especially if doing so involves potentially being attacked by a wild boar). The bottom line is this: our products can be great; our systems can be great; but if our staff aren't clear, or don't care, then they will not perform excellently, and our model for doing good (and doing well) will fail.

This chapter tells the part of AMK's story that relates to its culture, and how the organization worked to build clarity among staff, to enable them to do excellent work that balanced its dual objectives. To do so, AMK built a culture of learning and reflection, and a context where staff felt valued, to ensure that they were critically engaged not just with *what* they were doing, but *why*, as well as encouraging dialogue around *how to do it better*. For an organization trying to maintain a balance between value for clients and value for the business, innovation is key. Moreover, some of the best ideas for innovation come from the frontline, but only if staff are clear about why they're working in a certain way, and if they really care about doing a better job. Fostering these voices of innovation is crucial, and AMK did so by creating a culture where staff felt motivated and free to share their reflections, and supporting this culture through feedback mechanisms.

Creating a learning culture

From the outset, AMK labelled itself as a 'learning organization'; one which went beyond simply having a 'switched-on' management team that would review AMK's performance information behind closed doors and take corrective action as needed. The aim was to encourage learning at every level; to embed it in the very fabric of the organization's identity. AMK is a successful learning organization because it has built an institutional culture around encouraging staff to think about and engage with what they are doing in an active and constructive way, and to find ways of doing it better. After all, having thrown out its assumptions about what clients need, as well as conventional wisdom about how best to serve its clients, could AMK really assume that its staff didn't have new ideas about how to serve them better?

CEO Kea Borann puts the business value of AMK's learning culture into sharp relief:

> Employees are the ones actually spending time with the clients every day, and so they know best what the client really needs. If we motivate our staff to be fully engaged with their jobs and with AMK, they are able to innovate on processes and products and provide insights that can help Management, and that's a very powerful tool. We have a staff of nearly 1,500 people. If everyone has just one good idea each year – even if we only use 10 per cent of them in the end – then this is really useful for improving the way we are working.

How did AMK forge its identity as a learning organization? It did two interesting things: it fostered a culture of meritocracy (where the best idea wins), and rejected cultural norms around the concept of hierarchy (to encourage staff to share those ideas). Ly Theeda, AMK's first Human Resources manager, defined AMK's culture from the outset – not so much at a policy level as by setting the tone through example. Theeda explains: 'If we wanted to be a learning organization, we needed trust and communication. We needed to change ourselves first. We couldn't be arrogant with each other. In Concern it was not like this. This is something I built. Some people criticized me, because this was very unusual in Cambodia.'

We're going to need more chairs

As we conducted our interviews with former AMK staff, we heard an interesting story that really brought home the message about the importance of clarity and culture in terms of building an organization to do good. The story is about the Board-level Social Performance Committee (SPC). As discussed in Chapter 2, this committee played an important role in reinforcing AMK's clarity of vision, and brought to the table the facts and figures needed for AMK to take data-driven decisions in line with this vision. Olga Torres (former Research Director) likens early SPC meetings to marathons: typically lasting a full day and continuing on into the evening and dinner. As such, going to these meetings represented a big commitment for staff in terms of time away from both their desk, and pressing operational priorities. But what we found surprising about her story was *who* was actually sitting around the table. In theory, these gatherings were meant to involve only the SPC members, the Research Director, and the CEO – but the minutes reflect a much broader attendance. More often than not, the entire management team was sitting at the table, and often Board members too, because they valued the different perspective on AMK's work offered by the discussions, and the opportunity to critically reflect on what AMK was doing, why it was doing it, and whether it was working. For many, it was a unique opportunity to step outside the urgent operational details of their daily work, and focus on the bigger picture of AMK's work with its clients. The fact that people voluntarily gave up precious work time to engage in these conversations speaks volumes; if ever we were looking for an indicator that AMK's staff were committed to learning and improving, this was it.

Throwing out the hierarchy

If you want staff who will question the status quo, then you have to ensure they are not afraid to disagree with the boss. In the traditionally hierarchical culture of Cambodia, this is easier said than done. So how did AMK tackle this? If you were to enter an AMK branch office, or even AMK's headquarters, you'd be struck by just how difficult it is to determine who the boss is. Chheang Taing, the Chief Finance Officer, notes: 'What is different about AMK is the staff. In [other microfinance organizations], everyone wears ties, and senior staff wear jackets. Staff show respect for Senior Management by bowing their heads before speaking to them.' In contrast, everyone at AMK wears the same distinctive purple shirt, no matter what their job title. Taing continues: 'Everyone is equal, and we're happy about that. People do respect each other, but we all have the same rights. And I think that's correct – because at the end of the day, it's not about us, it's about the clients. We're here to serve them.' As a result, in the course of a branch visit, you may well see a driver sharing a table at a restaurant with a senior manager. When staff travel together, everyone gets the same per diem, and the same hotel – and will even share rooms.

This sense of equality among staff is underlined by the familiar style of address they use. Whereas in other microfinance organizations, respect for Senior Management is demonstrated by the use of formal titles, at AMK everyone – from Board members to cleaners – uses the terms 'brother' or 'sister' (*bong* and *oun*, respectively, in Khmer) to refer to each other. Newcomers to the institution often find this difficult to adjust to. Peaing Pisak (Head of Human Resources) reflects: 'When new staff arrive, they don't understand why no one uses honorific titles like "boss". To them it seems like no one is being polite to each other. We spend a lot of time instilling our open culture in our new hires.'

Creating a 'brother-and-sister' culture, based on commitment and respect, has helped AMK create an environment where constructive criticism isn't seen as a bad thing. Olga Torres (former Research Director) compares AMK's 'counter-culture' with local norms. She says: 'It's a cultural trait in Cambodia that people are not open to admitting their mistakes – saving face is much more important. In AMK, however, we don't hide from mistakes, and we're very open to suggestions. When staff had a comment, we responded, rather than ignoring it.' Being open to criticism is important at both an individual and organizational level. At an organizational level, a 2005 United States Agency for International Development (USAID) evaluation of AMK points to a culture of learning from mistakes, and an openness around talking about them rather than covering them up. Among staff, AMK's Human Resources department devoted significant effort to changing the mindset around staff performance evaluations. Peaing Pisak says: 'We tried to get [line managers] to focus not just on what their staff were doing well, but also what they could improve.' Along these lines, in 2011, AMK introduced 360 degree performance evaluations, where staff evaluate the performance not just of their subordinates, but their line managers too. This extends to governance level as well, with Management giving 'performance feedback' to the Board.

Creating a meritocracy

Of course, having a culture of openness, discussion and learning is of little use if people are not valued for the ideas that they contribute. For this reason, AMK developed a culture of meritocracy: where the best idea wins, no matter whose it is, and no matter what their job title is. This was important, but also radical: patronage and corruption are endemic in Cambodia. The 2013 Transparency International Corruption Perception Index[3] ranked Cambodia 160th out of 177 countries, and the most corrupt in the South East Asia region. In Cambodia, it is quite normal to get jobs and promotions based on family connections, or whom you know, rather than on merit.

In the context of AMK's work, the patronage culture implies a number of risks. Fortunately, at a macro level, the National Bank of Cambodia (regulating all microfinance organizations) is seen as a very effective regulator, and this is an important enabler for the development of the sector as a whole. AMK worked hard from the outset to challenge expectations around patronage in relationships with its clients. Microfinance is a 'pay-for-service' phenomenon, and the cost of that service is not a function of bribes or gifts given to staff. Under Concern, staff had been accustomed to accepting gifts from clients at village bank meetings – even simple ones, in the form of food or tea. AMK's Management worked hard to change this culture (through a zero-tolerance policy regarding gifts), and supported its positive messages with enforcement by internal audit staff, who included this aspect in their standard checks. At the village bank level, patronage-based relationships between clients within groups can interfere with those aspects that are designed to deliver social value for clients. Recall, for example, that the Concern programme ran foul of patronage when it found that clients' internal savings were being hijacked by the village bank president (often the village chief, who was more often than not the long arm of the ruling elite).

Within the broader context of the patronage culture (and by way of countering this culture at different levels), trying to convince staff that professional advancement was based on 'how you perform, rather than whom you know' was a tall order. Pete Power (former CEO) relates an anecdote that highlights this precise point:

> I was speaking with a member of staff who did not think he could apply for promotion as there was another candidate under consideration that was older. I said to him: 'But he's not as bright as you, and he's not capable as you. I want you to be the head.' The younger candidate was reluctant to even apply, even though I had basically told him I wanted to give him the job. He said, 'Oh, well, I have to think about that.' This kind of thinking is almost endemic in Cambodian society, but somehow Tanmay [former CEO] by and large has done away with this and created a culture that is a huge advantage, because it really empowers people.

Promotion within AMK is not based on seniority, and it is not automatic; rather it is based on individual staff member performance and education levels, as part of AMK's transparent Human Resources system. This system has taken effort to develop, and is particularly challenging in the branches; Management have heard complaints from staff where line managers have recommended people that they like, rather than the best performers. For this reason, AMK has integrated an interview and test process into the promotion decision matrix. Realizing, however, that some staff shine more brightly in interviews than on the job, AMK also takes into account recommendations from branch colleagues.

The battle to forge a new, meritocratic mindset within AMK is ongoing and not without its challenges, given that this is not the norm in many Cambodian organizations. There are still instances where Branch Managers rely on nepotism in making staffing decisions, or blame subordinate staff for their own mistakes. When this happens, Human Resources steps in to open a dialogue and support positive action.

Supporting the learning culture

If you're building a learning culture, equality and openness are a great place to start. AMK didn't stop there, though. It understood that it needed to bolster these 'mindset' aspects within its systems and processes. After all, creating a learning culture won't work if you don't have the right staff and management, with the right skills. And even if you find them, the culture will fail unless they stay with you in the long term, and feel motivated to make a positive contribution to your work along the way.

The leadership question

Cultural clarity starts at the management level and, from the outset, AMK developed a close-knit and motivated team. Pete Power reflects on AMK's early years: 'If you get the right people around you, you can generate an awful lot of loyalty – and you kind of have this sense of family loyalty, and the informality seen in a "start-up" culture. But nevertheless, [Tanmay] was very disciplined in terms of creating an intellectual thought process, and a strategy and business process – it was very well thought through.' Building on this foundation, Tanmay established a flat management structure from the start (in this respect, AMK has eschewed a more typical, top-heavy management structure which, having multiple layers, would make it difficult to move through them). When a CEO has the entire leadership team sitting at the table, and actively contributing new ideas and challenging each other's ideas in order to improve them, good things can happen. In recent years this has been reinforced with the creation of an executive team consisting of the CEO, Chief Finance Officer, and Chief Business Officer.

But it's not just having the right senior management team – it's having them stay with you for the long haul, so that the original vision can endure. Not only did AMK create a team that made sharing new ideas and questions the status quo but, by and large, the core people have remained in post (or advanced through the ranks) over the course of the organization's history. In 2013, for example, Management handed out awards to staff to acknowledge those who had given 10 years of service to AMK. The list was long: of the original 41 staff members, 30 were still there. This retention of senior staff (despite paying salaries that were well below industry averages) was a product not just of AMK's organizational culture and focus, but of the opportunity it provided for senior staff to develop in their own right as professionals, rather than being constrained by a top-down hierarchy.

Kea Borann (CEO) underlines the importance of this leadership longevity in enabling AMK to preserve its clarity of vision: in his view, the cultural DNA at the top of the organization was established early and maintained over time, and this has prevented AMK from repeating mistakes of the past. A newer member of the management team reflects: 'Overall, the team works closely together, and we support one another. But if I suggest an idea to change a policy, sometimes they will fight back – saying "we used to do that a long time ago (and it didn't work)".' On the flip side, the strong culture of questioning and reflection means that as new voices come to the table (new managers, for example, as AMK expands), the cultural disposition to consider new ideas is already in place.

So far, this sounds like quite a radical organizational vision. You might expect it to be the brainchild of one strong and charismatic leader, right?

Having spent a lot of time in the business section of various airport bookstores, we know that they invariably contain an ample selection of volumes analysing the strategic value of a charismatic leader to an organization (and how to become one in 10 easy steps). Clearly, leaders are important: individuals with vision and passion can set a strategic direction and motivate everyone to head for a far horizon. In the process of researching this book, therefore, we were on the lookout for that leadership dynamic. We pored over 10 years' worth of internal documents and interviewed every CEO, as well as a wide range of Board members, current and former staff, investors and other industry actors; and we fully expected to see an organization that was driven by the vision of the personality at the top. What we read, what we heard, and what we saw revealed, was that while getting the right CEO has of course been important, AMK's cultural identity has remained consistent, no matter who has come and gone. Certainly, each CEO brought their own unique strengths, weaknesses and styles to the table; yet AMK's organizational culture and focus have remained intact, despite having four CEOs in its short 10-year history – a fact that says much about its cultural resilience to change.

Having a clear and engaged management is important for nurturing a learning culture – and good communication with staff plays an important role in this. For AMK, it's not only about what messages staff hear from Management, but how they hear them. In this way, it's notable that in 2012, AMK's first Cambodian CEO took the reins. It has always been the intention to 'localize' AMK as an organization. At a management level, AMK hired two expatriates at the start (Tanmay Chetan and Olga Torres), but always planned to recruit Cambodians to these roles in due course (this happened sooner with the research function than with the CEO post, owing to a lack of suitable candidates). While AMK's culture is constructed in a way that isn't reliant on who holds the top spot, having a Cambodian CEO means that, for the first time, communication between the CEO and field staff doesn't need to be filtered through a translator. This is a huge asset in ensuring that the lines of communication are as clear as possible. Management meetings are also now conducted in Khmer, rather than English. At Board level, while taking on additional international investors means that English will remain the business language for the foreseeable future, having Cambodian nationals at the table means that the Board's decisions are informed by a real understanding of the local context, put forward by people who understand the relevance of particular trends or decisions from a Cambodian point of view.

Finding and motivating passionate staff

Every successful business needs to recruit and train the right staff, to do the right work, in the right way. But for AMK, transitioning from a not-for-profit to a commercial model meant that its staff had to learn a completely new way of working. Given AMK's dual objectives, this meant that staff needed to 'wear two hats' at the same time. For Concern's microcredit project, productivity was not an operational imperative. AMK's business model, on the other hand, required staff to work highly efficiently.

However, this focus on efficiency (supported through AMK's hard systems) cannot undermine the all-important staff-client relationship. Should clients run into problems, field staff need to have a real sense of what is happening in their lives, and respond creatively. For example, a client officer's ability to size up a problem and discern when a loan should be restructured (rather than chased for repayment) is critical for the social value model to succeed. So AMK doesn't just need skilled staff – it needs passionate, motivated staff who understand both what they need to do, and why.

So, how does AMK decide who qualifies? There's increasing recognition in microfinance internationally that the soft side – the passion for helping to create change in the lives of poor people – simply cannot be taught. Along these lines, when bringing new client officers on board, AMK focuses much more on a candidate's motivation, attitude and trainability than the skills they bring to the job. In fact, some staff join AMK as their first job on leaving secondary school.

Peaing Pisak, Head of Human Resources, says: 'For client officers, we require a high school degree at the very least. Prior experience is not a requirement. Then we give them two full months of training: some in the classroom, and some "on the job". During this time, we observe their commitment, and their willingness to work in remote rural areas, to work with poor people, and to work in an honest manner.' In short, through conversation and observation on the job by field-based management, AMK sizes up a potential new employee's ability to slot into its non-hierarchical culture of reflection and constructive criticism. All the while, the trainees are building their technical skills in doing sensitive work with the required excellence. Once hired, new staff are trained in how to speak to their line managers in a direct manner, using simple, clear communication and (importantly, given the local culture) eye contact.

AMK's emphasis on staff training dates from its inception as a business: its first strategic plan highlighted staff skills and morale as a potential management risk – and identified on-the-job training as critical to mitigating this risk. In this way, AMK invested considerable resources into capacity building from the start. (Contrast this with the approach more commonly seen across the industry, whereby organizations are scaling back staff training in the name of efficiency, despite the potential for such training to contribute to both increased quality and productivity.) One of the first tasks assigned to the Training, Research and Marketing department (TRAM) in 2003 was to establish operational procedures (and create the didactic material) required to enable staff to work effectively and consistently. Not only did this involve training for new staff, but also 'refresher' training for credit officers already in post. During this time, the Operations and Finance departments did a great deal of close mentoring and providing on-the-job guidance to new staff. In early 2005, these efforts were consolidated with the establishment of a Human Resources department. Although this 'coaching' approach weakened somewhat during the period when the 'cracks' formed (discussed in Chapter 3), it remains a strong driver at AMK today, perhaps even more so than formal, structured training sessions. Importantly, senior staff still play a large role in mentoring junior staff, and all department heads at AMK are trained in the 'soft skills' involved in giving and receiving feedback. This interaction is an important way of connecting junior staff with the 'big picture' of what AMK is doing and why, and giving them an insight into Management's priorities – so that they aren't just learning what they need to do, but why they need to do it.

Looking after staff is looking after clients

Getting the right people with the right skills on your team is clearly important. But once they're there, how do you get them to stay? And do you want them to stay because there's no better employment option, or because they are genuinely motivated and committed to their work? When it comes to doing difficult work, staff motivation is an important driver of excellence, for two reasons. Firstly, well-treated staff will in turn treat clients well, and will be more willing to undertake the difficult tasks demanded by the business model. Secondly, the longer staff stay, the more they learn, and the more that their organization reinforces this learning through ongoing mentoring, the more that investment in training will be paid back.

When we talked to staff, it was clear that many of them had been drawn to AMK precisely because it is an organization that does good work. Upon arriving in 2012, Chheang Taing (current Chief Finance Officer) reflected:

> The feeling of AMK was right, something was bringing me here. When I was young, and living in the province, I always felt that I wanted to help the poor. It is my pride to be working with AMK. I came from a bank where the mission is to be the leading commercial bank, which is less motivational. What has impressed me the most is going to the field after only a couple of weeks working for AMK – when I was with that bank I never went to see the clients. I see that AMK is completely different, that we are serving our clients, and I am very impressed by this.

However, when it comes to asking staff to make a long-term commitment to difficult work, there are real limits to the extent to which you can rely on altruism. Staff might understand what they need to do and why, but where is the motivation to go the extra mile? In those same conversations with field staff, when we asked them why they *stayed* at AMK, the organization's vision and culture around poverty-focused microfinance was always second on their list. Their first response? That they felt well looked after by the institution. This is not the story of a mission-driven charity staffed by individuals willing to make personal sacrifices in the name of social progress. They also want to feel valued (in tangible ways) for the work that they do. Yes, AMK is an inspirational place to work – it is doing important, innovative, and exciting things – but it also needs to be a *great* place to work.

For this reason, AMK has put a lot of time and energy thinking about how best to look after its staff. This is quite rare, given the Cambodian context of relatively poor labour rights, and often exploitative conditions for lower-level staff of organizations. This commitment is reflected in its salary structure (see Figure 4.1), which is competitive at lower levels (and interestingly, less competitive for senior posts – a good indication of how committed these individuals are to the whole AMK project). Benefits also play a key role here, particularly given that AMK's work is relatively more difficult than that of other organizations in the market. Indeed, when speaking with employees, they are quite vocal in expressing that they perceive AMK's benefits to be better than those offered by its competitors (even if those competitors *do* have nicer offices, as discussed in Chapter 3). In fact, when the new head of Human Resources joined in 2012, she was surprised to learn that AMK's benefits were also better than those of the large international NGO that she had just left. AMK's medical insurance, for example, covers all costs for staff members as well as their families; other standard features of the benefits package include accident insurance, paid holiday, weekends off, overtime pay, and an annual '13th month'/Khmer New Year bonus pay cheque. At first glance, having a great staff benefits package might seem like altruism on the part of AMK. More to the point, however, it recognizes that the risks staff face while doing difficult work (in terms of their health, wellbeing, or impact on time with family) often run counter to their ability to do excellent work.

So what is the result of this focus on staff? While AMK achieves relatively low levels of staff turnover (currently around 13 per cent, which is favourable internationally, and on a par with some of the stronger organizations nationally), of course not all staff are happy. Since 2005, AMK has conducted a detailed annual staff satisfaction survey that provides Management with information essential to understanding and improving the employee experience; this is segmented by length of service, role within the organization and gender. The survey is strikingly positive in relation to the big picture of AMK: 85 per cent of staff are positive about the overall company strategy (mission, vision, principles, strategy) and, when asked about the working environment, more than 80 per cent of staff are positive, with less than 3 per cent negative. The survey also highlights the challenges of day-to-day operations, with some areas of dissatisfaction around Human Resources policies and working conditions, particularly among client officers, and some issues around branch management. Overall, 37 per cent of staff have thought about leaving the organization in the past year, mostly for reasons of workload or career progression opportunities (although only a third of these actually left).

Table 4.1 AMK salary benchmarking against sample of Cambodian microfinance organizations

Level	Job titles	Average salary from sample ($/month)	Average AMK salary ($/month)
Level 1	Chief Executive/Operating/Finance/Business Officer	4,504	2,982
Level 2	Heads of department and senior managers	1,724	1,224
Level 3	Deputy heads of department and managers	934	781
Level 4	Unit managers	573	733
Level 5	Senior officers	358	434
Level 6	Officers	223	327
Level 7	Assistants and tellers	184	232
Level 8	Drivers, Clerks	183	202
Level 9	Cleaners, Guards	172	148

Source: Market study commissioned by AMK, 2013

Strengthening learning systems over time

In the early days, when the organization was still comparatively small, AMK's learning culture was strong, partly due to Management prioritizing this aspect. A more formal infrastructure to promote feedback developed over time – and indeed is still in development.

Certainly the role of the Research department, as well as the critical questioning and reflection role that the SPC has come to play at Board level, has been of great historical importance in holding AMK accountable to evidence-based decision making. The culture of openness, critical reflection and learning is certainly strong at the head office level, and is supported at the organizational level through formal systems for feedback and input; however there is some variation in how this culture has seeped into the daily work of staff at branch level and where perhaps the culture is more hierarchical. This learning ethos was also seen to ebb somewhat during the period of rapid growth, when Management gave less attention to innovation, and the imperative was not just 'business as usual', but 'lots more business as usual'. Especially as staff numbers swelled to handle greater numbers of clients, the challenge of translating the culture message from head office to operational staff became a real challenge.

Looking back, it is clear that in the years before the financial crisis, growth became an end in itself rather than the product of quality. As we discussed in Chapter 3, this revealed cracks emerging in operations and provided AMK with an important wake-up call: that growth could not come at the expense of operational excellence and a mission-focused staff. The organization had become very centralized, with nine people reporting directly to the CEO, and the sense of openness and meritocracy had been somewhat eroded. Salary scales, for example, had been removed from the Human Resources policies and had come to be considered confidential. Aspects of Human Resources that had previously been emphasized, such as ensuring a gender balance, had been neglected; the internal audit team, for instance, had grown to 17 men, with no women. The focus on learning from clients had also weakened.

In the wake of this, as discussed earlier, Management focused a lot of energy on strengthening the hard systems that framed the work of its staff (such as incentives). Beyond this, it also took steps to formalize AMK's learning processes and bolster its questioning culture, to ensure that staff priorities were pointed in the right direction, and that the conversation around 'what are we doing as an organization?' encompassed not just growth, but growth with quality. That is, it recognized that if loan appraisals weren't being done correctly, or if individual loans were being pushed too much, then simply tinkering with management systems would not automatically bring staff into line. Staff needed to understand *why* these things were important in terms of the bigger picture of what AMK was trying to achieve and how. This, then, needed to be part of the message, and part of the ongoing conversation within the organization. And if things were going wrong, staff needed to recognize this, and bring their perspective to the table.

Pete Power, who stepped into the role of CEO in 2010, played a big role in strengthening the culture by spending a lot of time out in the field with staff, both to engage in dialogue and promote learning. A number of organization-wide events, such as an annual retreat and a biannual Open House Forum in each branch, where Management meet branch staff, are attended by all of the head office management team. These fora are structured with the aim of bringing staff closer together (no small challenge given the size of the organization) and sharing insights on what's working, and not working, within AMK. AMK has also recently strengthened mechanisms for staff to give direct feedback through a variety of means: staff satisfaction surveys; feedback boxes; a 'whistle-blowing' hotline (the records of which are only accessible to the CEO and the Risk Department); as well as the 360 degree appraisal process. These efforts have been bolstered by significant investment in staff training and management team development.

Building the right Board to deliver value

Understanding; skills; good attitudes; motivation. Having all of these at the staff and management level is critical to achieving excellent work – and the same applies at the governance level. The Board is ultimately in charge of defining and overseeing issues around strategy and quality, so it needs to have a clear and balanced vision of what the organization is trying to achieve.

For AMK, the development of the Board is rooted in the story of the organization's transition from an NGO to a for-profit company. So, how did AMK ensure that its Board brought the skills and perspectives it needed to manage its dual objectives? Critically, this story is not one where the parent organization (Concern, in this case) made a quick exit once the ink was dry; indeed Concern's long-term involvement with AMK was a critical factor in maintaining the latter's focus on clients. In the early years, there was a tangible anxiety that becoming a for-profit organization would lead to a dilution of its social mission. Yes, AMK needed to succeed within the marketplace; however, it was essential that this did not come at the expense of its focus on reaching poor clients, understanding their lives, and making balanced decisions on that basis. Having the right governance was essential.

While a lack of business acumen at Board level was identified as a key risk factor in AMK's first strategic plan, what's interesting about AMK is that it deliberately pursued a Board diversification strategy to balance the social and commercial perspectives. The Board needed to be 'social' enough to maintain the mission focus and 'business' enough to develop the systems and processes required to operate on a commercially successful basis. AMK thus recruited individuals from the formal financial sector to the Board, as well as local experts conversant in Cambodian legal, corporate and taxation issues, as a means of adding depth to the Board's knowledge around operating in the local industry environment, especially in the context of new and evolving microfinance regulation. Importantly, too, bringing on non-Concern representatives was seen an important strategy for attracting future debt and equity investors, in that being seen as a single shareholder organization might have made AMK a less attractive investment.

Over the years, AMK took quite a measured approach to this diversification strategy. There was no rush to fill the boardroom to the rafters with bankers and lawyers; rather, AMK sought to ensure that new Board members who brought commercial acumen to the table shared the organization's vision for delivering social value, and were prepared to invest significant time in contributing to strategic decision-making. Acknowledging that potential new Board members would be more motivated to associate themselves with AMK once it had established a real market presence and 'brand value', the Board decided to wait for a year before bringing on any non-Concern Board members – and to wait for two years before seeking external input from significant numbers of others. Reflecting on AMK's Board diversification strategy, Pete Power notes: 'It was a nice Board; not an NGO Board by any means, because we had a bunch of banker people on there. There were a lot of different perspectives; perhaps the Board was bigger than it needed to be, but over time I think the two halves, the social and commercial, learned an awful lot from each other.'

For AMK, having the right people on its Board was critical to ensuring clarity around its social and commercial objectives. It also took important steps through the SPC to ensure that the client perspective was present in Board-level discussions, and that this conversation translated into effective strategic and operational decisions. In practice, this meant putting facts and figures on the table to make 'mission passion' a tangible thing, and building the skills of Board members to analyse and understand data and relate to AMK's work on the ground. Olga Torres reflects that in the early years (when the Board was still dominated by Concern staff) she directed a great deal of effort towards teaching Board members how to read a basic business balance sheet. In later years, as the Board increasingly became populated with individuals who had banking, business, or law backgrounds, Board training was focused around unpacking questions such as 'what is poverty?' Throughout, Management also arranged Board field visits to ensure that its members met staff and clients, and had a real and abiding sense of exactly what AMK was trying to achieve, how, and for whom.

It's important, too, not to overlook the importance of the Board chair in providing the link between the Board and the CEO. When this relationship works well, it means the right balance of strategic guidance and management autonomy. For AMK, it was also important that the Board chair, in particular, embodied the vital balance between the organization's social and commercial priorities. Theresa McDonnell Friström (the Concern Cambodia Country Director) took on this role for the first two critical years when AMK was building its foundations. Having been involved in the Concern microcredit project, her social value credentials were not in doubt, but she also had the foresight to create the space that allowed AMK to develop as a commercial entity, independent of Concern. From 2005 until 2010, the Board was chaired by Tom O'Higgins, a senior PriceWaterhouseCoopers professional, who was also an ex-chair of the Concern Worldwide Board. This blend of corporate and charity sector experience provided a solid grounding in governance and finances, combined with an understanding of and commitment to the social mission needed during AMK's period of rapid growth. During these key years in AMK's development, Tom played an important role in guiding both strategic decisions, and the relationship with Concern. Back in Ireland (at Concern's headquarters), Tom's word was taken very seriously, and he was the biggest factor behind Concern's unswerving support for AMK, even as the latter's rapid growth prompted increasing questions about the relationship between the two organizations (see Chapter 6). Since 2010, Tanmay Chetan (AMK's first CEO) has assumed the role of Board chair, in his capacity as the representative of AMK's largest investor, Agora. While his intimate strategic and operational knowledge of the organization is, of course, valuable, it had the potential to create the risk of overstepping the line between the strategic guidance of a Board and the operational decisions of a CEO. However, the solid foundations of a core of long-standing Management and Board members, and a history of good working relations, have served to outweigh this risk, and there is a strong and constructive relationship between Board chair and CEO.

Overall, AMK's diligence in creating a balanced and skilled Board has paid real dividends: it has created a system of internal check and balances that contain any pressure to adopt a more commercial approach (although, like the rest of the organization, the Board had a wake-up call following the financial crisis, which led to improvements in its systems after 2010). The clarity the Board has demonstrated in managing the delicate issue of loan size is an important example. As mentioned previously, poor clients are the least likely to clamour for larger loans. Within AMK, it is actually the field staff who are the most vocal advocates for loan size increases. Management tends to put the brakes on these decisions by maintaining a focus on the needs of poorer clients, and considers the matter carefully before taking it to the Board, which has made clear that gaining approval for larger loan sizes will not be easy. In 2014, Management put forward a proposal to increase group loan limits from $250 to $375, based on detailed client feedback and business analysis by the Research department. The Board, recognizing the risks to clients of over-indebtedness, opted for a cautious approach and declined to approve a nationwide rollout, instead insisting on a pilot test in a few select locations.

Looking ahead

In Parts I and II of this book, we've discussed two essential ingredients for becoming an organization designed to do good: getting your products right and getting your people to reflect your vision in their work, backed by ongoing critical reflection as they carry out that vision every day. In Part III, we'll set these two aspects in motion, and discuss what it takes to combine them into a business model that works for both your organization and your clients – and how this needs to adapt to a changing landscape over time.

Notes

1. As a result of this, and a large-scale write-off of bad loans, portfolio at risk (an indicator of late repayments) was brought down from 3 per cent at the end of 2002, to 0.71 per cent two years later.
2. A phrase coined by Danny Miller in his 1990 book, *The Icarus Paradox: How Excellent Companies Can Bring About Their Own Downfall,* New York: Harper Business.
3. The Corruption Perceptions Index ranks countries and territories based on how corrupt their public sector is perceived to be. A country or territory's score indicates the perceived level of public sector corruption on a scale of 0–100, where 0 means that a country is perceived as highly corrupt and 100 means it is perceived as very clean. A country's rank indicates its position relative to the other countries and territories included in the index. The 2013 index includes 177 countries and territories. For more see www. transparency.org/cpi2013 [accessed 3 September 2014].

References

Dasgupta, S.; Poutiainen, T.; Williams, D. (2011) *From downturn to recovery: Cambodia's garment sector in transition,* Turin: International Labour Organization Available online: http://www.ilo.org/wcmsp5/groups/public/asia/ro-bangkok/ documents/publication/wcms_189460.pdf [Accessed 26/11/2014].
Sinha, S. (2013) 'Microfinance in Cambodia: Investors' playground or force for financial inclusion?' [online paper] Gurgaon: M-CRIL. www.m-cril. com/BackEnd/ModulesFiles/Publication/Cambodia_Analysis_1_2013.pdf (December 2013) [accessed 26 August 2014]

PART III
Building a business model that works

This book is about building a business model for good. In Parts I and II, we've explored the 'products' and 'people' angles: how we can shed our assumptions, do our homework, and design products and services that respond to clients' needs. We've talked about how to operationalize that understanding of 'what works for whom' in the way that we monitor and improve the work we do. We've also explored why quality delivery is not automatic (especially in light of the tensions inherent in a social enterprise model), and how we can put in place hard and soft systems to shape the path towards quality, and tap into considered insights for innovation from frontline staff. All of this is about not missing opportunities to do good (or more good) within the marketplace, and protecting clients from harm. In short, it's about making a social enterprise work from clients' perspective. But what about making our work 'work' from a business perspective?

As we touched upon in Part I, the access question is important for organizations of all types. Even the best product, with the best delivery mechanism, will come to naught unless the business model enables clients to access the product in the first place – where and when they need it (and for as long as they need it). For charities, access comes down to convincing donors (or the general public) that a product is socially valuable. The more funds you can raise, the more money you have to deliver your product where it is needed. For commercial enterprises, access is a matter of business value: testing products in the marketplace, and striking the right balance between price and cost, in order to deliver them at a profit.

What, then, does access look like for social enterprises? Yes, social value is important, but the financial model must also make sense. In the case of AMK, we have an organization committed to changing lives, and an overriding imperative to make the maths work – something which was particularly challenging from the perspective of what AMK was trying to do, where, and with whom. In this way, AMK presents us with a catalogue of innovative business model decisions, which map out some interesting issues that other social enterprises can interrogate when figuring out their own 'sustainability maths'. For some organizations, this will simply be a matter of covering operational costs. For others, it will be about profitability. Either way, without a lasting presence in the marketplace, the organization will fail to deliver long-term good. So, in the case of AMK, what did the maths look like?

http://dx.doi.org/10.3362/9781780448640.004

Choosing the dirt road

AMK set out to be a pioneer along a literal and metaphorical dirt road that was unmapped, and untested. It wanted to do two things, and do them well: design and deliver products to poor rural people that would make a difference in their lives, and become a financially profitable business. The latter in particular was essential if it were to raise the capital required to achieve massive scale. Had it listened to conventional wisdom, it would not have believed this to be possible at all. Indeed, most other microfinance organizations at the time built their business models around serving moderately poor urban dwellers, who were less costly to reach (and in theory, less risky to serve). AMK set its sight on rural areas, where poverty was highest. Rather than listening to the voices of doubt about whether this could be done sustainably, AMK started with its goals and principles, and built its business model to deliver on these. The charity Concern's support of AMK in its early years (see Introduction) played a big role in making this happen; not only in terms of financial backing, but also in providing the continuity of governance that encouraged AMK to push the boundaries of possibility.

To make the maths work, AMK needed to balance high costs with increased efficiency, productivity, and client loyalty. It needed to achieve economies of scale, and at the same time acknowledge its own limitations. Being cost-effective and highly efficient meant that an overly ambitious range of complex products and services was out of the question. Within its offering, AMK also streamlined its methodology to the bare minimum, without losing sight of what mattered. At the same time, it had to achieve a level of profitability that would make it attractive to investors in order to access the capital so essential for expansion (note here that even so-called social investors usually expect commercial levels of return, although they are less risk averse and tend to provide long-term support, rather than looking for quick returns).

AMK succeeded in finding a business model that worked for what it was trying to achieve. But this is not to say that its focus on doing what was right for clients always made immediate business sense, or that there were no trade-offs involved. What makes AMK's experience valuable to a broader social enterprise audience is the importance of examining your trade-offs, and weighing up those trade-offs over a timescale that makes sense for you.

On paper, going deep into remote rural areas was more costly. AMK's priority was to make this work, while recognizing that it was incurring higher costs. Over the long term, it has found that this business strategy has worked very well. By tapping into areas untouched by other service providers (given that the competition, by and large, stayed in the towns and cities), AMK had a captive market within which it could expand rapidly, and leverage that outreach as it expanded its offering. In practice, it discovered that far from being more risky, reaching out to poorer, more vulnerable clients resulted in increased client loyalty, and a lower risk of default (provided products were designed appropriately). Moreover, as AMK expanded into less remote areas over time, the costs reduced. It has started to leverage its market-leading position in client outreach and diversify the products offered, thus creating huge opportunity, both in terms of delivering more value for clients, and in financial returns. This is evidenced by AMK's first commercial equity investor having joined the Board in 2014.

In the long run, therefore, a challenging, socially motivated outreach strategy has not only proved to be a realistic business model, but also to make good business sense. While this is partly luck, of course, and has not been without trade-offs, the key insight to draw is this: we can define our own trade-offs, rather than accepting everyone else's.

An evolving business model

Breadth, depth, efficiency, complexity. These are the variables that AMK has juggled to find the 'sweet spot' between its commercial and social objectives. That said, the decisions that a social enterprise takes about what to do today will differ from those it takes five years into the future. What changes? Simply put – everything. Our clients change. Our internal capacity (human and technological) changes. The external environment changes; regulation, competition, the political environment, and even public opinion, all influence the way that our work evolves over time.

As such, AMK's experience provides a perspective on the idea that 'what our business model looks like' is not a one-off. The landscape in which we operate is in constant flux, and our business model must evolve over time. The story of AMK runs parallel to the story of dramatic economic and social change in Cambodia, and the explosion of the microfinance market. The opportunities available to clients have changed, and with them their expectations and demands on AMK. Where we fail to account for internal influences and external forces, we run the risk of our business model quickly becoming obsolete.

In the 11 years since its inception, AMK has evolved from a largely credit-only business into a multi-product, multi-channel provider of financial services (including non-credit products such as micro-insurance, remittances and savings). The essential understanding of the potential role that these services could play in helping clients meet their varied financial management needs has been there from the start, but the evolution of AMK's response to those needs has been, in large part, down to balancing what it offers with its internal capacity and external context. Again, scale was important. An essential precondition for a sustainable move to a more intensive, multi-product focus was for AMK to establish a huge market of loyal clients to whom it could offer those services (working intensively with a smaller number of clients might not have held the same profitability potential, given the investment costs).

In terms of the external enabling environment, regulatory issues meant that products such as savings and microinsurance were often 'in the works' for a long time before AMK was allowed to launch them. Chapters 5 and 6 consider how AMK's approach evolved over time, and how it made its business model work for the people it wanted to serve.

CHAPTER 5
Insight: Own the dirt road

'What can you do to support AMK's social mission?' That was the first question that they asked. The National Bank of Cambodia is responsible for maintaining the integrity of the financial sector, as well as its reputation – and this face-to-face meeting with our potential new investor is an important step for us when we bring on board new capital. When we arrived, we fully expected the National Bank representative to ask our new investor about capital adequacy and whether they were looking for a quick profit, or were making a longer-term investment. What we were expecting less, and were pleasantly surprised by, was that they started with our mission instead. The official said: 'We are very proud of AMK's social mission, at a time when some other microfinance organizations are trying to become commercial banks and might not be so interested in their social goals. How would you, as potential investors and shareholders of AMK, preserve and strengthen its social focus?' It was a great question, for two reasons. Firstly, it was heartening to see that the central bank valued more than just financials in AMK. Secondly, the new investor had decided to invest in AMK precisely because of its strong social footprint. It felt like the ideal meeting of minds between the regulator, management and shareholders of the institution. Of course, the questions on capital adequacy, long-term commitment and on finding more Cambodian investors were also on the agenda. However, the lasting impression from this meeting was that the central bank understood and valued the aims that AMK pursues, and did not want new shareholders to dilute this emphasis of mission. We felt very reassured after this meeting.

Tanmay Chetan (Chair of the Board, AMK)

What is so remarkable about this story? For us, it's the message emerging that AMK is doing something remarkable as an organization. It took its social value proposition and proved that it could be socially beneficial and financially viable at the same time. In doing so, it threw out one final (and big) assumption: that sustainable poverty outreach (of the order it was trying to achieve) simply couldn't be done. Rather, AMK started with its social mission – to reach out to poor people in remote areas – and built a business model that worked to address the challenges inherent in doing so sustainably. Yes, it was important that it understood its clients' needs, that it delivered good products with quality, and that it improved those products as it went along. But the question of how to make it work from a business perspective went much deeper.

Fundamentally, AMK had to define its relationship with growth. To do so, it started training a social value lens on key business model questions: who to target; how many clients it would reach; what it would actually do, as a business, about meeting its clients' needs; and what it would *not* do. This meant grappling with issues around the potential trade-offs and synergies inherent in its business model, such as: 'how can delivering more valuable services reduce the risks and costs we face?'; 'when is a valuable product or service too costly or complex to manage?'; 'how can we offset our higher costs in the way that we approach our work?'; and 'how much can we push growth without damaging the staff-client relationship and the quality of delivery?'

Reflecting on Tanmay's story, the influence that a new investor has on an organization is potentially massive; to us it is striking that the National Bank was interested in the relationship between AMK and its potential new investor, not just in terms of its financial impact but its social impact. More to the point, since the National Bank didn't want AMK to become 'just like other organizations in the marketplace', why is it that AMK's vision was seen to be so remarkable?

In some ways, the answer can be found in a history lesson. Back in 2003, when AMK was incorporated, a war was afoot in the global microfinance industry. The questions up for debate were whether microfinance organizations could reach poor people sustainably, and indeed whether poor people could effectively use financial services at all.

At war with conventional wisdom

If there were no market failures, there would be no need to challenge the status quo. What we mean is, social enterprises strive to move beyond business as usual and create a different model to correct for market failures, reshape market forces, and address gaps that undermine the interests of poor and excluded people. Microfinance began by challenging the conventional wisdom enshrined by the commercial banking sector, that poor people were un-bankable because of the high costs associated with lending to them (these costs were driven by the fact that loan sizes were very small, that the borrowers lacked collateral to secure loans, and that they often lived in hard-to-reach areas). The innovation that microfinance brought to the table was to identify this pressing need, overcome access barriers, and create a viable means of extending financial services to this previously excluded segment of society.

However, the question of 'how deep do we go?' remained. Put simply, the issue up for debate was: 'just how poor does a person have to be, to be too poor for microfinance?' Was there diminishing marginal social and commercial utility in reaching out to increasingly poor segments of society? Indeed, despite the sector's revolutionary beginnings, the majority of microfinance institutions quickly imposed limits on how far they pushed those boundaries. When AMK was incorporated, conventional wisdom for most part held that there was a direct and automatic trade-off between commercial success and poverty outreach. In essence, the goal-posts of exclusion had merely shifted, rather than disappeared; while it was no longer the case that poor people were considered un-bankable, there were serious doubts that the same could be said of very poor people.

This presumed dynamic between commercial success and poverty outreach in microfinance was neatly encapsulated in a line graph, describing an inverse relationship between the two. Performance against both of these objectives could (within the curve) be optimized – but only up to a certain point, when the inevitable trade-offs started kicking in. Around this worldview, two warring 'camps' quickly formed within the microfinance industry, soldiered by practitioners advocating for one or the other to take strategic precedence as the industry grew and matured. According to the 'financial systems camp', the poorest of the poor were beyond the reach of profitable microfinance delivery; they were best left to organizations doling out charity (which perhaps, to a certain extent, reflects an implicit discomfort with the concept of profiting from the poor). For those in the 'poverty camp', reaching the poorest of the poor was a moral and ethical imperative; anything less was a betrayal of the ideals that microfinance was created to serve. Theresa McDonnell Friström (chair of the Board, 2003–2004) described the impact of this 'war' on her own views: 'During the transformation process I experienced first-hand the sustainability/poverty "war" within microfinance. Up until that time I would very definitely have been aligned with the so-called "poverty camp". But my experience of the war made me question my beliefs.'

For readers outside the microfinance sector it seems important to stress that, for both sides, there was a lot at stake. This was a debate about the very identity and future of the microfinance industry, waged fiercely in journal articles, conference plenary sessions, and in the development of different business models for financial service providers. To say that this debate was heated is not hyperbole; a quick internet search reveals impassioned pleas in major journal articles by prominent thinkers in for calm and respectful dialogue[1] between the two sides.

Putting the debate under the microscope

At the risk of stirring up old passions, it seems useful to put this debate under the microscope for a moment. If the trade-offs were absolute, then what the line graph was *really* describing was a lender's appetite for the presumed cost of lending money out – and the presumed risk that they wouldn't get their money back. Within this, there was a value judgement to be made: was simply increasing financial inclusion an end in itself (irrespective of depth of poverty outreach)? If this were the case, then simply targeting the 'low-hanging fruit' in urban and peri-urban areas (the so-called 'entrepreneurial poor') in large numbers would be sufficient, and outreach to the poorest of the poor should be pursued only if it were commercially viable (and valuable) to do so. In any case there was a consensus that very poor people would be unable to use credit productively (and more importantly, repay it).

This was a contentious issue, as seen in the uproar (from the so-called poverty camp) when one influential donor body, in 2003, changed its name from 'Consultative Group to Assist the Poorest' to 'Consultative Group to Assist the Poor'. For the poverty camp, mission fulfilment was directly related to how poor clients were, not just whether they were formally excluded. The underlying belief was that very poor people *could* make productive use of credit, and a certain degree of subsidy was justifiable to help reach them.

With the benefit of hindsight, our perspective is that these two worldviews were based on an incomplete understanding of the relationship between sustainability and poverty outreach. Firstly, at the time when this debate was raging, the industry still lacked the tools needed to ensure that very poor people could be reached effectively, and that the products and services they were offered were well adapted to their needs and, importantly, did not increase their risk and vulnerability; most organizations provided one-size-fits-all credit-only offerings. Secondly, and more importantly, the relationship between poverty outreach and sustainability is more complex than just loan sizes; lending costs and risks are not the only variables that influence whether an institution is sustainable.

Pulling more levers

Repayment rates, portfolio at risk, and client loyalty all have big roles to play in the dynamic between poverty outreach and sustainability. For AMK, serving poorer, harder-to-reach clients was certainly more costly in the short term, but there were also upsides. Higher costs-to-serve were partially offset by a level of client loyalty that is comparatively high for the sector (and less staff time spent chasing overdue loans). This resonates with international experience, which shows that poorer clients tend to repay more faithfully (perhaps because they have fewer options in life and value continued access to credit), and are more likely to turn into repeat clients. Also, for AMK, it wasn't necessarily true that less-poor clients were a lower-risk investment. AMK found that by delivering a large number of small loans, it could spread the risk of default.

Going after easier-to-reach clients can also be more costly from a client protection perspective: more accessible clients are more accessible *to everyone*. This means more competition, more risks of over-indebtedness, and ultimately a higher cost for the institution in establishing more time-intensive and costly methods to assess credit repayment capacity and protect against over-indebtedness. By going to remote areas, AMK was able to operate free from competition in its early years. That said, as we explained in Chapter 1, poorer people are more vulnerable (with fewer and less reliable income sources, and lives that are susceptible to shock). For a lender to adapt its services to the needs of very poor people, and ensure it doesn't cause harm, it must make a deliberate investment in product design and learning; therefore, AMK invested heavily in research. Anything less than this, and it would be reckless to target very poor people. Certainly, then, there are nuances in terms of whom an institution serves, how it serves them, and how risky or costly an investment this is. This is especially true when an institution's risk horizon is expressed over a longer timeframe, and when we add other factors, such as competition (or lack thereof), into the mix.

What strikes us about the experience of AMK is that by asking a few more questions, and pulling a few more levers, it was able to challenge the myths that very poor people were out of the reach of microfinance, and that they couldn't be served in a sustainable way. The line graph described trade-offs that were automatic and absolute; AMK set out to push those boundaries. What precisely did this involve? Well, AMK started with its two core objectives: delivering social value, and becoming commercially viable as a business. It built a business model around these that made the maths add up.

AMK's 'outside-in' strategy

If you look at everybody else, they started out from the main roads and then they expanded from there. We actually went to the most remote areas and started working our way back in.

Pete Power, (CEO) of AMK, 2010–2012

AMK came to the market armed with a strong focus on poverty outreach. In the economic landscape of Cambodia at the time, this meant heading out into rural areas. We talked briefly in Chapter 3 about the pressure on staff created by AMK's geographic focus, and it's worth revisiting that point here. The remoteness of those areas, and the time it took to reach them, was the main implication in terms of cost. The 120 km journey between the Bantey Meanchey and Siem Reap branches (both in major towns in the north of the country) today takes one and a half hours; in 2003, it took *no less than six*. These were areas without roads; without access to markets; where malaria was rife; and where, in some areas, people had very little practical experience with the concept of money. For example, one client officer we interviewed related the story of a client in his group who wanted to buy two bottles of cooking oil; upon arriving at the shop he bought them one at a time, in two separate monetary transactions, rather than purchasing both in one transaction. Moreover, security for client officers (travelling long distances with cash) was a real concern, given the high levels of gun violence and robbery that continued to plague the country after years of turmoil. Once there, client officers were delivering very small loans (averaging US$38 in 2003) to clients with low levels of economic activity. These were the challenges that AMK faced in terms of building a business model to achieve sustainability. As Gerhard Bruckermann (who, as a financial supporter of Concern, joined the Board in 2004) reflects: 'Our poverty focus did ask for economic compromises. We knew that we were going into areas that were financially challenging. The option of going upmarket, though, was never on the table, because of our strong focus on the mission.'

The targeting question

Managing the financial costs inherent in simply getting out into rural areas was challenging enough, but once it got there, AMK needed to grapple with fundamental questions around how best to attract and serve poor clients. It certainly wasn't left to chance: AMK's current outreach methodology is the result of careful debate, deliberate design, and close monitoring over time.

So whom did AMK target? And where did it come down on the question of 'how poor is too poor for microfinance?'? In its early years, it decided to target the 'economically active poor' – but not for the reasons you might think. Here, too, a bit of history is useful. In the years up to the registration of AMK, three successive Concern Country Directors rejected proposals from the microfinance programme management team to shift its target client upmarket from the poorest to the economically active poor (which, on the face of it, seemed like a move towards less-poor clients). Internal research seemed to support this decision, highlighting that some 32 per cent of clients had no income-generating activity at all. However, when AMK's research department moved the focus from individuals to *households*, they found that there were in fact multiple sources of household income, and this changed the analysis of clients' ability to productively use and repay a loan. The second realization was that it wasn't a clients' poverty status that mattered; it was their cash-flow, and whether this was significant enough to absorb a loan. After all, in countries such as Cambodia where there is no social safety net, even the poorest of the poor (the destitute, or beggars on the street) need to be economically active in order to survive. It's all a question of degree. This was part of the discussions, and in 2005 there was consensus that if beggars had enough income to repay loans, they could become clients. Given this, internal consensus favoured a shift towards targeting simply the poor, rather than being precise about how poor clients should or should not be.

Having defined whom it would serve, the next question was how to distinguish these people from non-clients. At the time of its incorporation, AMK had the option of inheriting Concern's direct poverty targeting tool (used to ascertain individual poverty levels on entry), but declined to do so, for three reasons: efficacy, efficiency, and (interestingly) ethics. Firstly, in practice, Concern's (well-intended) poverty targeting methodology was, partly through lack of proper oversight, riddled with mismanagement and fraud. It incentivized clients to disclose only partial information about their income and living conditions, and incentivized staff to cut corners with targeting and to blame their clients' poverty for repayment problems. Secondly, recognizing the challenge implied in a business model that targeted clients in hard-to-reach areas with very small loans, any process that could safely be dropped from the client officer's 'to do' list would only increase AMK's efficiency. Finally, the ethical dimension: from the outset, AMK's Management felt a certain level of unease with a top-down process for deciding who got loans and who didn't. That is, AMK designed its loans to meet the needs of poor clients, but stopped short of predetermining exactly who could access them, placing a higher priority on freedom of choice and non-discrimination.

Having rejected a tool-based approach, AMK's belief was that, by being present in areas with the highest incidence of poverty, and designing its products to meet the needs of poor people, it would encourage the poorest segments of society to self-select into its programme. As part of this, careful management of loan sizes has been a cornerstone in AMK's poverty targeting methodology. At the outset, group loans were capped at $50 for the first cycle, with an increase of $25 per subsequent cycle available up to the maximum limit of $125, subject to repayment capacity (determined through cash-flow analysis). Management's position was that small and tailored loan sizes gave clients the capital they needed without putting them at risk of default – and that overly rapid growth in loan sizes was a signal of mission drift.

Beyond the arguments around targeting and client protection, there is an institutional perspective that favours smaller loan sizes. As discussed in Chapter 3, AMK's data shows that, unless the required expertise for effective assessment and monitoring has been developed, larger loans carry more risk. Significant loan size growth would also put pressure on social cohesion within groups, as clients would be responsible for guaranteeing larger and larger loans for their peers. The visible result of this was that AMK's average group loan sizes were significantly lower than its competitors; AMK has consistently had the lowest average loan size among microfinance organizations lending in the rural areas.

So did this strategy actually work? To find out, AMK began collecting poverty data annually from a sample of new clients. This gives it an overall picture of whether it is staying on track with its poverty outreach goals. Interestingly, AMK does not set a specific poverty outreach target. However, it does look at poverty outreach at an organizational level, and compares this with national poverty level data. This is important, because it allows AMK to put its poverty outreach into context. That is, if a trend is seen in terms of the poverty outreach for new group clients, this can be compared to national trends to see if it is likely to have been driven by internal or external factors. All in all, AMK's data demonstrates its success in reaching poor clients. In fact, looking at the comparative poverty data, we can see that for a number of years, when AMK was pushing into rural areas, its poverty outreach deepened even while national poverty levels were falling (see Figure 5.1).

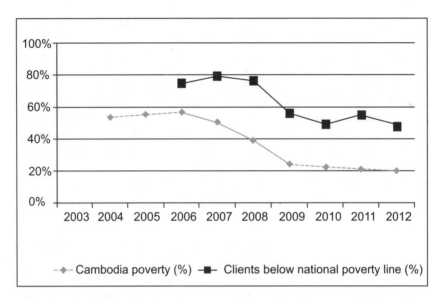

Figure 5.1 AMK's outreach to poor clients compared with national poverty trends, 2003–2012
Source: 2013 AMK Change Study, 2014

However, tensions at the operational level remain that could potentially translate into exclusion of poor clients. For example, we found that the idea of reaching out to the economically active poor rather than simply the poor still has some currency among field staff, who believe that less-poor clients are a better investment. In a performance-orientated organization, there will always be a tension between the mission and productivity, and it is natural that staff feel risk-averse towards accepting clients whom they feel might give them future problems. As we discussed in Chapter 4, this is a challenge that Management addresses on a day-to-day basis by affirming the mission, and coaching staff to understand the rationale and efficacy of AMK's strategy.

Making the maths work

While AMK's strategy of offering small loans in remote rural areas might have reaped dividends from a social value perspective, from a financial perspective it meant a business model based on high operating costs and very small potential returns from any one client. There was a drive towards keeping other costs as low as possible, but without cutting corners. As such, senior staff salaries are relatively modest, as are AMK's headquarters and branches. Large capital expenditures such as technology upgrades were made with care and an eye on cost, and there is also a real consciousness among staff about avoiding waste (e.g. turning out the lights on leaving a room). However, streamlining overheads alone could do little to balance the costs of rural outreach.

Returning 4x4 cars to Concern

AMK inherited a fleet of nine cars which were used for moving cash between the head office and the branches, and one for the exclusive use of the CEO. It retained one for each of the three branches, one for head office, and returned the rest to Concern. The 'red car', which was retained for head office staff to use when visiting the branches, is still in service in Phnom Pehn, 11 years later.

The report of the Concern Cambodia Transport Management Consultancy concluded in September 2002 that 'an independent microfinance organization would not be able to maintain the major capital replacements of 4x4 vehicles which is currently supported by Concern'. It calculated the cost per km to be between 24 and 30 cents, including depreciation costs, and the annual transport running costs of the three Concern branches to come to a total of over $24,000, not including 'internal' maintenance costs or depreciation. This equated to the annual interest paid by 1,550 village bank members on their loans; or to 18 per cent of AMK's interest from the 8,700 clients who remained among those AMK had inherited from Concern, once it had cleaned up the portfolio. Translating this figure into real costs for real clients served to highlight the inefficiency of this expenditure.

We can see this dynamic playing out when we compare the operating expense ratio of AMK and its competition over time. This ratio is a company's cost of doing business (expenses) divided by its loan portfolio. The lower the ratio, the more profitable a company will be: it makes more for every dollar it spends. Where a company can increase its income *without* a commensurate increase in relative expenses, then that is an indication of the scalability of the enterprise.

AMK's operating expense ratio – its cost of doing business – has fallen significantly over time, from 49 per cent in 2003 to 19 per cent in 2013. This is due to a combination of improved infrastructure (roads, running water, telecommunications); achieving economies of scale and efficiencies in the business; and the lowering of costs as it has expanded into less remote areas. While most microfinance organizations in Cambodia achieve similar or lower operating expense ratios, it is notable how much higher the ratios were historically for those organizations focused on rural outreach.

At the start, however, AMK's very high cost-to-serve ratio for clients meant that serving them sustainably was a challenge. Part of AMK's thinking around what to do when it arrived in rural areas involved recognizing that its poverty outreach strategy *did* affect its financials, certainly in the short and medium-term. Not that the organization was unprofitable, but its margins were lower and more fragile (especially in the face of widespread economic shocks, as discussed in Chapter 3), so it needed to work harder and be more efficient (that is, it needed to be a stronger organization than its competitors to reach the same levels of profitability).

The cornerstone of AMK's response was to build economies of scale into its business. In this way, it was able to balance low margins with high volume. Interestingly, growth is often seen as embodying risk in relation to social value: risk of an overriding focus on profit, a consequent loss of focus on target clients (read here poor clients), and a loss of service quality. In essence it is seen as tipping too far towards the commercial end of the spectrum. However, when we say that AMK aimed to be the biggest microfinance organization in Cambodia in terms of client outreach (but not in terms of portfolio size), we understand that this growth was a means, not an end and, importantly, a means to both positive social and positive financial outcomes. With respect to the former, it was the means to increase impact through reaching ever more clients, especially those in remote rural areas. Regarding the latter, 'going big' was the only way to make any headway in the context of low profit margins. As former CEO Pete Power muses: 'finding the "sweet spot" was the only way to make this whole crazy proposition work'. In this way, both the social and commercial aspects of the organization were aligned within the focus on growth.

Linked to achieving scale, AMK staff were asked to achieve very high levels of productivity. As the organization expanded to reach every district in the country (and as many villages as possible within those districts), field staff aimed to serve as many clients, in as little time, as possible. This meant that lengthy one-on-one attention for individual clients was not an option. Client officer portfolios grew from 539 in 2004 to an average of 937 in 2006. This was high for the region,[2] and very high compared to global averages. The bottom line was that AMK field staff worked very hard indeed, and had very little individual contact time with each village bank member.

Did this translate, however, into purely superficial impact for clients? Did high productivity targets mean that AMK's products and services delivered less value than they might have? Not necessarily. AMK balanced the tensions created by its strong efficiency drive in two ways. Firstly, good product design. It did everything it could up front to ensure that clients succeeded, thereby creating savings for AMK in terms of future problem-solving. Appropriate loan sizes and terms, based on cash-flow analysis, that met clients' needs – all these things, that AMK did to generate social value (see Chapter 1), had real financial payoffs as well. Secondly, methodology. Key features in AMK's lending methodology (such as the role of the village bank president) helped to ease the burden on staff in terms of paperwork and problem-solving, group formation and management. The fact that village bank presidents knew their fellow villagers, and lived in the area, meant that problems were identified and addressed as they arose, not just when the monthly village bank meeting took place. In this way, clients received the ongoing advice, encouragement, and support that they needed; it just didn't come from the client officers themselves.

However, AMK's rural and poverty focus did not only involve costs. By being the only financial service provider in the area, it was able to avoid some of the impact of competition. As Paul Luchtenburg (former CEO) recalls: 'Being the first mover in new areas did have one advantage in that there was less competition in the unserved provinces.' Recognizing that it's less expensive to keep old clients than to train new ones, AMK also seeks high levels of client satisfaction and loyalty through well-designed products and services (based on solid research), and close management of delivery quality. When we compare AMK's retention rates with the competition, there is evidence that AMK's approach has worked: in 2012, AMK's average retention was 82 per cent, compared with an average of 62 per cent from a sample of organizations in the sector.[3] These rates tell us the extent to which clients were struggling, failing, or dissatisfied. Training new clients is smart – both in making sure that they're using their loans in a way which directly benefits their livelihoods (social value), and that they are able to repay them (commercial value). Smart, and costly. In this way, AMK had every incentive to make sure that clients succeeded and stayed in their programme, to ensure that it was recouping that cost over the medium term, rather than losing it in the short term.

Evolving over time

While AMK's early focus on remote regions might not have made immediate commercial sense, it did afford the organization the space it needed to grow rapidly without pressure from its competition, and establish its reputation within the market; dividends which it is now reaping. The outside-in strategy made sense in the context of high levels of productivity, to balance the high cost-to-serve ratio for each client. Over time, AMK's internal calculus around productivity targets has changed. This is due partly to the more cautious approach it has pursued since the financial crisis, and the cracks that started appearing in its individual lending approach; but it is also due to the fact that, as competition increases and AMK moves into less rural areas, pushing productivity is no longer possible, and neither is it desirable. In fact, client officer average portfolios dropped from their peak of 937 in 2006 to 746 in 2008, falling as low as 522 in 2010 and 2012. In part this reflects the reality that it is harder to recruit new clients in a competitive environment, but it also creates space to spend more time with each client, and to use that time to deliver a range of other services that are valuable to poor clients. In this way, AMK is still applying a deliberate approach to product design in order to attract poor clients.

Maintaining a focus on poor people

Do we grow with our clients?

Broadly speaking, AMK's strategy of heading into rural areas and offering small loans was successful in attracting poor people into its programme. However, it's also important to recognize that poverty is not a static thing. National poverty levels change, as do client needs. In this way, an organization needs to grow alongside its clients – and an important part of this is increasing average loan sizes over time.

From a poverty outreach perspective at the industry level, a swift knee-jerk reaction to the subject of average loan size increases was not uncommon in AMK's early years. In the absence of reliable poverty measurement tools, bigger loans were seen as synonymous with mission drift. But rather than accepting this at face value, AMK's leadership started asking questions such as: 'At what point do our small loan sizes no longer meet the growing needs of our clients?' and 'At what point is our focus on small group loans (albeit very large numbers of them) no longer financially viable?' Former CEO Paul Luchtenburg strikes upon another relevant issue, linked to the fact that clients' livelihoods continually develop: 'If AMK isn't keeping up with inflation, then in real terms it is actually giving clients smaller and smaller loans over time.'

In this way, decisions to increase group loan size limits were the outcome of considered discussion. Automatic loan size increments (in place at the start) were replaced with increments based on a cash-flow analysis (after the first loan cycle). Maximum limits have similarly increased, but with a more rigorous cash-flow analysis, from $38 in 2003, to $150 and $250 in 2007 and 2010, respectively – still much lower than the competition. This doesn't mean, however, that caps are overly low: AMK has historically allowed its average loan sizes to increase at a rate that exceeds inflation. This reflects a general reduction in national poverty levels, as well as its expansion into less-poor areas (for example, the Board approved a 20 per cent increase in the loan size caps in early 2014, as an inflation adjustment). Today, group loans are capped at $300, and individual loans at $2,500.

Of course, there's a delicate balance here: if group loan sizes grow too large, then it will quickly tax the group guarantee mechanism (whereby no physical collateral is required to secure a loan; social collateral between members means they will hold each other to account for good repayment behaviour, and help each other financially when repayment problems arise). Secondly, within the context of lending to vulnerable clients who are susceptible to income shocks, there remains a natural limit to the risk which AMK can reasonably accept in offering larger and larger unsecured loans.

A close brush with mission drift?

Growing with clients is also about recognizing that, ideally (in theory as a result of income growth supported through access to credit), clients will in time outgrow the small loan sizes on offer as part of the village bank groups. This was a large part of AMK's thinking behind the introduction of the individual loan product. The initial idea was to offer this as a 'graduation' product to group clients with steady and growing income streams (who might otherwise have left AMK in favour of other providers as they started springing up in the rural marketplace). Later, AMK would open it up to a wider, more entrepreneurial (read, less poor) segment, once it understood market demand and preferences.

It should be noted that there was a certain amount of hesitance at Board level to the idea of individual loans, especially from Concern representatives, who were strong advocates for a focus on poorer clients. The decision to proceed was linked to a cap on individual loans of no more than 10 per cent of clients; this would mean that 90 per cent of AMK clients remained rural poor. This essentially came down to a recognition that AMK needed to define on its own terms what mission drift meant for it as an organization. It was not about loan sizes, nor about having individual loans, but about failing to reach its target clients; and AMK's data had proved that it had successfully penetrated the poor end of the Cambodian marketplace.

There was also a commercial dimension at play here. Diversifying the portfolio away from poorer clients in similar and vulnerable income-generating activities (primarily rain-fed agriculture) meant spreading AMK's risk across different client groups. The business case was outlined in the 2004 strategic plan:

> Floods have affected the Concern microfinance program regularly in the past, and have resulted in sizeable portfolio losses during the last two years. A primary reason for this has been a very high exposure (close to 100 per cent) on loans for rice production in the past … new products to match the cash-flows of non-agriculture activities are likely to be a viable option in most villages and even more so in semi-rural areas and rural markets.

As discussed in Chapter 3, AMK's first attempt at an individual loan product was not well managed. Apart from the impact on portfolio quality, the rapid growth in individual loans led to a significant change in the profile of clients. AMK does not track the poverty level of individual loan clients, but it can be safely assumed that they are well above the poverty line. A concern for mission focus, combined with the problems experienced with bad debt, led AMK to return to a more cautious approach to individual loans. While recognizing their value to clients for expansion of a business or farming, it limited their number, introducing a 10 per cent cap as a percentage of client portfolio. While competitors have moved increasingly to individual loans, AMK has remained committed to working with groups, seeing this as a key part of its ability to reach out to poorer people with uncollateralized loans.

Over time, AMK has seen a significant decline in the percentage of new clients living below the poverty line: a fall from 79 per cent in 2009 to 56 per cent in 2009. This corresponds with AMK's expansion inwards, away from the most remote areas, to include larger towns and cities. As this 'repatriation' process unfolded, the internal and external landscape changed radically from AMK's earliest days.

But was this really mission drift? At the same time as AMK's poverty outreach was declining, so too were overall poverty rates in rural areas. In fact, rural poverty rates had dropped to 39 per cent, and national poverty levels were down to 35 per cent. Given that AMK's poverty outreach was

56 per cent, it was clear that it was still reaching people who were much poorer than average. In this way, AMK's poverty outreach remained broadly consistent with its mission to reach poor people, even though it was experiencing a trend towards reaching better-off clients in absolute terms.

This dynamic highlights why AMK rejected operational targets or benchmarks for poverty outreach, and why it prefers to have an ongoing discussion on poverty trends, portfolio trends, and the impact of market saturation. This approach allows the organization to take a more nuanced view about whether it is improving over time, and to understand why the numbers might be moving in an unexpected direction. Given the rapid decline in national poverty levels, setting benchmarks would have been akin to aiming at a moving target.

Looking ahead

By defining its own trade-offs, and its strategy to overcome the operational challenges inherent in its social mission, AMK has grown to be a major player in the marketplace. It has achieved a level of scale and internal capacity (in terms of skills, technology, and processes) that can now be leveraged as the organization diversifies. In recent years, AMK has moved from an extensive model that focused on outreach to as many poor people as possible, to a more intensive approach that seeks to deepen value – for both clients and the institution. While the rest of the microfinance sector has (following the post-financial crisis slow-down) returned to high portfolio growth rates, AMK's portfolio growth is significantly lower: 25 per cent compared to the sector average of 50 per cent in 2013.

Chapter 6 looks at how AMK's diversification is driven by its continued focus on delivering value for its clients. We will explore how, over time, the strategy for this has evolved and changed to reflect an understanding of opportunity and risk for clients, internal capacity, and the changing environment in which AMK operates.

CHAPTER 6
Insight: Adapt to the changing landscape

I have a good shop. Maybe not the biggest in the village, but I am in the centre, which means that people pass by often. My customers know me and like me, and I sell them what they need. They come to buy candles, or soap, or airtime – some vegetables too. My cousin grows them, and I sell them on her behalf. I also sell little sweets for children at festival time. I can give my customers advice, too. Many of them are members of my village bank. I have been president of the village bank for almost two years now, and it's my job to help them when they're having problems. And when they do, they always know where to find me, any day of the week. I am good with numbers, and I can read a little, and I always find a way to help them. So you see? I am an important part of the community.

I was proud when AMK asked me to help them with a new idea – they came to me six months ago, and said they wanted me to be an agent for their new savings and transfer service, as a new service that my shop could provide. I thought it was just what they needed to do. Some members of my village bank had AMK savings accounts, but to be honest they didn't use them very often. You could only save money at the monthly meeting when the credit officer was there – or in between meetings, if you travelled as far as the branch. But this new mobile service – my customers can deposit a little money when they come to buy their flour. Or if they need to buy medicine in a hurry, then they can come and withdraw savings from me, any time my shop is open. Even if it's not, they all know where I live, and I'm happy to open the shop late when they need me to. They can even use the phone that AMK gave me to send money to their family living in different provinces.

And now in addition to giving advice to my group members, I have new jobs. I tell my customers about the products, I help them open an account and give them their special card to use in my shop, and I collect information about customers to give to AMK when they open their account. Each time someone makes a transaction I get a fee – not very much, but if lots of people start coming it could add up. So I tell everyone that comes into my shop about how they can start an account – even if they don't have an AMK loan. I keep a special box with my own money in it – at least $50 – so that whenever customers need to withdraw, I always know that I have what they need; if it runs low then I have to call the AMK officer to bring more money. Of course, I am proud to have the AMK sign on my shop, because they have given me loans that have helped me expand my business. But I am disappointed that more people are not using this, and that I am not making money as I had hoped. It took a long time to learn how to use the mobile service, and how to explain to people why they should open an account, *and the different ways they can use it. I heard that another agent opened in the next village, but after a few months she is shutting down, because no one comes to her either. But I won't stop. I wish I didn't have to keep so much of my own money in the box – but I trust that in time, the savings business will pick up, and it will be worth it.*

Ut Sreypov, Toul Krasang village, Saang district

If we could travel back in time and have a conversation with AMK's Management on the very day after they were incorporated as a company in 2003, they might not actually believe us if we mentioned that 10 years down the line, AMK would be offering mobile savings and transfer services through third-party agents. Of course, the essential recognition of clients' need for savings has existed from the outset; and in following AMK's journey over the years, we see the different ways in which it has tried to respond to that need. At first, it offered direct savings services through village bank meetings, but then realized that, within the limits of regulation and technology at the time, it couldn't deliver the type of savings that clients needed: savings that could be accessed in the village at any time. At the point at which Sreypov's story unfolded, during the pilot phase of agent banking in 2012, AMK hadn't fully cracked the business model. It had started by making its services work for clients' needs, and had built the model around this, but hadn't quite considered how to make them work for the agents themselves. We'll explore later in this chapter how AMK adapted the model to make it work for both clients and agents.

The path that AMK has taken to make agent banking really work highlights the challenges of developing a business model in the ever-evolving landscape that surrounds social enterprises. Over its 11 years, the world around AMK has changed quite dramatically, and AMK along with it. As such, this is a story about an organization whose internal capacity was changing: its capacity to deliver complex services, and its ability to leverage its size in order to do so effectively. It is also a story about external factors such as a growing economy, changing regulation, and grasping the potential offered by new technologies, new partnerships, and even changes linked to clients themselves as their livelihoods and expectations have expanded. As competition increased, AMK needed to not only offer products, but also to offer products that were attractive when compared with those offered by competitors, and with a higher level of customer service. As one credit officer[4] relates: 'If we don't treat our clients as king, then they will go to another provider.' Finally, then, this is a story about AMK making its mark within a competitive landscape of other financial service providers; adjusting its needs-driven approach as clients enjoy increasing access and choice between providers; and seizing the first mover advantage in new products and services.

This changing landscape comes replete with new opportunities, and new risks, for businesses striving to do good, and do well, within the marketplace. Where we fail to respond to these, we risk making our organizations obsolete, missing new opportunities to add value to the lives of our clients, or even doing harm when the old model doesn't work anymore. Guiding a social enterprise through a changing world means having to grapple with a number of questions, such as: 'what is our role as an organization within the broader ecosystem of service providers?', and 'when is it right to "think outside the box"?' Organizations taking a product-driven approach tend to stay within the confines of that 'product box' – but AMK's needs-driven approach has led it to recognize a broader set of needs that require more than just credit. The business case for offering savings and remittances was not straightforward, however, and AMK had to make quite a radical change in whom it worked with in order to build an effective business model. Our next changing landscape question is this: where a needs-driven approach leads us to recognize a broader set of social needs, where are the outer limits of our model in terms of how we respond? That is to say, just because we see a need, does it necessarily follow that we should try to respond? Finally, how can we stay attuned to external influences that require us to completely change the way we're working, even if we were happy with the original model?

This chapter brings together all the threads we've been developing in the course of this book: how to build an organization that responds to its clients' needs and delivers on its promises, and how to make the business model work from the perspective of its social mission. AMK does not have a set of innovations that can be replicated. Rather it demonstrates how a clear vision and understanding of need has guided its decisions over time, as it has constantly adjusted and evolved its way of working. As we learned in Chapter 5, AMK's initial business model juggled variables related to breadth, depth, efficiency, and complexity to find the sweet spot between its commercial and social objectives in order to deliver credit to poor rural communities. Over the following 11 years, AMK evolved, moving closer to its vision of delivering a suite of financial products and services that would meet its clients' diverse needs. This evolution required AMK to grapple with three of our changing landscape questions; leading it to expand its offer in line with changing capacity and context; think through its role in terms of meeting a broader range of social needs; and adjust its credit approach in the face of increasing competition. This chapter will look at these developments in detail.

In all of this, it's important to remember the financial imperative to make the business viable, and how the concept of viability changed over time. AMK's vision was always a level of growth that required external capital to achieve, and, therefore, the levels of profit to attract that investment. In this way, it was asking more than: 'can we achieve a level of productivity, efficiency, and portfolio quality which means that we can cover the cost of operations?' Instead, it asked: 'how can we achieve a level of profitability that will also allow us to pay interest on loans and attract equity investors who seek a good financial return?' Proving the financial viability of the model from very early on was therefore important.

It's worth highlighting that the radical changes accompanying AMK's transformation into something more than a credit-led business are still very much a work in progress. However, a recent equity investment by a commercially focused investor indicates that AMK's balanced vision is a compelling one. AMK's outreach strategy has created a platform to deliver a range of additional services to its clients. Apart from the potential social value for clients that this implies, it also represents a significant commercial opportunity. The new investor eschewed investments in other microfinance organizations that give higher short-term returns on equity based on expectations of future value. For the investor, a focus on client value makes sense as the means to build commercial value. Thus, while there have certainly been trade-offs in the past, AMK's future prospects seem to offer a win-win business and social value case.

Financing growth: moving from charity to investment

Growth posed financial challenges, and demanded adjustments in the relationship between AMK and Concern. Up until 2007, most of AMK's needs were financed through Concern by a private philanthropist (Gerhard Bruckermann). However, in light of rapid growth – the loan portfolio grew from $840,000 in 2003 to over $23 million by the end of 2008 – additional money was needed. Concern did not have this sort of money, and became increasingly alarmed by the size of this financial liability on its books. Rather than the usual charity project, which eventually comes to an end, AMK represented an ongoing, growing financial asset that needed to be managed; neither did Concern have the financial expertise to manage commercial borrowing. Paul Luchtenburg, the then CEO, remembers this time well: 'When I was there Concern had little experience of borrowing from serious lenders. I remember one loan of $200,000 which involved an excruciating seven-layer process, going up almost to Concern Board level.'

The process of setting up loan agreements for AMK (which had to be approved by Concern) highlighted the challenge of aligning the processes of the two organizations. Pete Power (Board member and former CEO) recalls negotiating a loan during his time at the Concern headquarters. The lender would only give a definite interest rate two days before the loan was signed; Concern, however, needed a week or more to thoroughly review the loan agreement, which had to include the interest rate. To break this stalemate, an interest rate was agreed at midnight with the lender. Pete then spent the next day going from office to office to go through the loan terms with key people in Dublin so that the agreement could be signed the next day.

These delays put AMK's business model at risk, and also created the risk of lack of liquidity which could compromise its capacity to make promised loans on time: one of the most damaging things for a microfinance organization, particularly in a competitive environment. It was clear that further separation of the two companies was needed. This led to a decision by Concern to bring on board other shareholders and, eventually, to Concern's decision in 2008 (formalised in 2011) to sell its holdings in AMK to a new social investment company (Agora) led by AMK's first CEO, Tanmay Chetan. A Concern Board member explains that this may also shed light on why Concern did not try to replicate the experience of AMK in other countries: its commitment and support to AMK was critical in building its successful poverty-focused model but, generally, charities shouldn't be running banks.

Balance what you offer with capacity and context

Context and capacity matter when it comes to defining a business model. In light of what AMK was allowed to do (in the regulatory sense) and its drive to serve as many clients as possible in its early years, it examined the full picture of its clients' needs and made a strategic decision. To start with, it would only respond to *some* of those needs. AMK chose to focus on working extensively (reaching large numbers of poor people with a slim product offering) rather than working intensively with smaller numbers (with a wider range of services to meet a broader set of needs). Thus, at the outset, AMK focused on credit only (although in a way that was aligned to those needs and avoided putting clients at risk).

Interestingly, some of AMK's earliest choices about what to do around its credit offering hinged on the question of its own organizational cash-flow. The availability of guaranteed capital funding from Concern in the early years was of crucial importance, as AMK was able to experiment with products in a way that might not have been possible within the constraints of lender funding. The successful credit line product encountered a lot of resistance because of the seemingly unpredictable nature of draw-downs and repayment (in reality it proved much more predictable than originally anticipated). However, most lenders require regular instalments of capital repayments, so without the grant funds from Concern, this product might have been a non-starter. Even with the product in place, AMK experienced resistance from potential investors who considered the product risky.

More recently (having achieved scale, with increased market competition providing less scope for an extensive approach) AMK has begun to leverage its size (in terms of number of clients) and to work more intensively through new credit products, plus a suite of non-credit financial products, to meet a range of other financial management needs. Far from seeing any trade-offs on the financial side of this intensive approach (associated with increased costs for development, training and marketing), AMK is starting to see real synergies. Working intensively means that it understands the needs of each client better and is positioned to cross-sell its range of products to meet those needs, which leads to greater value for clients and increased revenue for AMK. There are also pay-offs in terms of client retention – particularly where the competition *isn't* offering those particular services. Some product concepts were in the works for years before the regulatory framework allowed AMK to pursue them. Others came on line as technological barriers fell away, or, as in the case of non-financial services, the concepts changed as AMK found better ways of making them work from a business model perspective.

Today at AMK, we see a real enthusiasm for innovation as it rolls out, pilots, or discusses many new products and services. The constraint of the credit-focused model is gone, and AMK is exploring new possibilities driven by both client need and business opportunities. As a result of a new deposit-taking licence, AMK was able to introduce several new products and delivery channels, including a mobile savings product and domestic transfers (remittances). Another significant development lies in AMK's efforts to develop a microinsurance product to cover health and accidents, which represent clients' most pressing risks. Having been granted an insurance licence in early 2014, AMK has started to pilot the product through a partnership with a commercial insurance company.

The dangers of standing still

If this chapter is all about creating a business model to balance value and harm within a changing landscape, then the evolution of AMK's response to multiple lending provides an interesting insight into what this looks like in practice. The key driver in this story is increasing competition for clients, as the microfinance market has become more saturated in a short space of time. AMK's outreach strategy initially focused on remote areas with little competition. Today, the Cambodian microfinance market has matured, with high levels of geographic coverage leading to significant overlap between providers and differentiation of these providers in terms of their target markets. This new competitive landscape forced AMK to re-think its approach to multiple lending (both from a social value perspective, and from an avoiding harm perspective).

We talked in Chapter 5 about the crucial role that small loan sizes play in AMK's poverty outreach strategy. They make sense both in terms of client needs and in terms of not exposing clients to over-indebtedness. But what happens when a client wants access to more credit than AMK is willing to offer and takes another loan from a different lender? AMK's response, again, has been to err on the side of caution. Prior to the establishment of the credit bureau (in 2012), AMK's policy forbade lending to clients with outstanding loans from other microfinance organizations. In the absence of reliable information, however, this was sometimes hard to verify. Client officers relied on the honesty of clients (and their neighbours or guarantors) about whether they had another loan. Internal audit, spot checks by Management, and field visits by staff to talk to the local community, all played a key role in trying to establish the facts. It must be said that other financial service providers did not feel the same compunction to prohibit multiple lending. Thus, when the credit bureau was launched, AMK saw that approximately 20 per cent of its clients had other loans. At that point a strict policy (based on credit checks) was enforced: if a client borrowed from another lender, they could not borrow from AMK.

However, this approach did mean that AMK was (at a policy level) excluding potential clients, especially as market saturation increased, and AMK found itself competing with five or six other lenders in an area. New clients with other loans were barred from applying and sometimes clients were forced out in the middle of the loan application process if they took another loan in the interim. One client officer recalls the tensions inherent in this: 'I had a bad experience in penetrating one market because of the competition. One village bank had 12 groups, but when I arrived I could only disburse to two of them, as the other 10 had taken loans from other lenders since they had joined AMK. According to the policy, I had to reject them.' Could AMK really afford to lose increasing numbers of clients in the name of avoiding over-indebtedness? And could AMK really afford not to grow in an increasingly crowded marketplace?

Irina Ignatieva (SPC and Board member) reflects:

> For a long time, the Board didn't let go of the 'one client, one loan' policy. There was a lot of pressure from Management on this particular one, as the competition was so stiff, and there were so many people in our operational areas; if we didn't lend to clients that already had loans, there would be no more growth. So the challenge was perhaps to make peace with the fact that there is such a thing as market saturation and competition.

For a social enterprise, it all comes down to which variables are within your control, and which are not, and shaping your response in recognition of these factors. AMK knew that it could not influence the lending practices of other microfinance organizations, nor could it prevent clients from wishing to borrow more if offered the choice. However, where clients wanted to borrow more capital, it was infinitely preferable that they do so from AMK rather than the competition, given that AMK was so strongly focused on delivering value and avoiding harm.

Accordingly, in 2013, in response to client exit analysis highlighting this issue, AMK implemented a cautious policy allowing some multiple lending, using cash-flow analysis to calculate appropriate debt levels up to a maximum of $500 for group clients. Nevertheless, even with credit bureau information, lack of real-time information about a client's debt meant that this was far from perfect in its implementation.

Recognizing that it would be less risky (for the client and AMK) if AMK could base its loans on a full understanding of client debt, and that the clear demand from clients might in fact represent a genuine need, AMK's Board agreed early in 2014 to a policy of 'internal multiple lending'. This allows clients to take an additional loan from AMK based on a careful cash-flow and debt analysis. Clients with a good track record and adequate capacity can now take on a second individual loan from AMK for an additional economic activity, up to a maximum of the equivalent of $125 (500,000 Cambodian riel). Ideally, this will serve to limit clients' exposure to other lenders, whose policies are less strict (and potentially less geared towards protecting clients from harm). In theory, it should also decrease AMK's risk of default: where clients borrow from multiple institutions and subsequently run into trouble, the crunch factor is where the client decides whom to repay first. Generally speaking, client officers have good relationships with clients, and based on this, they estimate that approximately 60 per cent of multiple-loan clients would repay AMK first. However, where other lenders have harsher collections practices, there is every incentive for clients to repay AMK last.

The issues of cross-financing and the risk of over-indebtedness are a concern for Management. If loans are correctly assessed, and clients understand and act on their financial situation and ability to repay, then in theory there's no problem. So building client understanding and financial capability is clearly desirable. In this way, AMK is currently exploring how to incorporate strategies to build client financial capability, with a separate team looking at options such as delivering training sessions in group meetings or through a partner organization.

Exploring the limits of the product offering

We mentioned earlier in this Chapter that, for the first nine years of its existence, AMK was by and large a credit-only organization (notwithstanding a small uptake of voluntary savings, which will we discuss shortly). This is true in terms of purely financial services, but there's more to the story than that. After its initial period of innovation, AMK had a solid set of workable credit products, and focused its energy on taking them to scale rather than developing new ones. However, the core understanding of clients' broader needs, highlighted through AMK's livelihoods research, never disappeared from the radar.

Poverty, after all, is not just a lack of money. It is a multidimensional beast, manifest in a lack of access to clean water, reliable electricity, good health, decent education, numeracy, literacy, adequate shelter, voice in the political process, or in a lack of protection from social and political violence. All of these affect a poor person's fundamental ability to provide for their family. Once we recognize this, we can identify external constraints that limit the impact of financial services, and opportunities to add further value through other services. Indeed, in recent years, there has been increasing focus within the microfinance industry on 'bolting on' additional non-financial services to help clients address these wider needs; specialized financial products for niche markets are also the product of such thinking. From the point of view of a social enterprise trying to balance client and institutional priorities, the question is then, what is the organization prepared to do about these issues within its business model?

AMK's experience of responding to these needs and getting its fingers burned (so to speak) was an important learning experience and led to a strong push from the Board for AMK to focus on doing what it does well: providing financial services. During a short period (2009–2010), AMK's Management proposed a number of niche financial products as well as complementary non-financial products. These included:

Solar lamps and water filters. AMK aimed to use its distribution channel to sell products (at cost) that would benefit its clients, namely solar lamps and water filters. These were sold through five complementary non-financial service officers acting as sales representatives for the companies in question. Top-up loans to purchase these products were unavailable at the time, but were under consideration for the future.

Loans for vulnerable groups, such as victims of trauma and human trafficking. These were to be very niche, socially focused products, taking up only a small proportion of the balance sheet (for example, AMK made only 17 loans to vulnerable trafficked women in its first year).

While these products might have been closely in line with AMK's social goals in terms of helping clients improve their livelihood options, the business model did not fit with AMK's principles of scalability and financial discipline. There was also a cost in terms of reputational risk to AMK, and the management time that was absorbed in forging the links (and often preparing donor funding applications) to support and manage these activities. Projects were pursued opportunistically, mostly responding to available donor funding rather than to detailed client-level research. Broadly speaking, there was interest but concern at Board level. The issue was approached with great caution, both in terms of the financial and reputational risk to the organization if clients were not happy with these products, and whether AMK as a financial service provider was best placed to deliver them (as opposed to specialized NGOs).

On reflection, we see that the Board was right to take a measured approach, given the poor fit between AMK's initial approach and its overall business model. In this respect, as with other issues, the financial crisis came at just the right time for AMK. With a spike in bad debt and client exit, the Board called a halt to these projects, instead focusing on addressing the cracks in quality that had appeared in its financial service offering. As Irina Ignatieva (SPC and Board member) notes: 'I think [at the start we were] socially minded, but in a different way. There were special project departments, and special products. This was good, but it wasn't very business minded.'

Wider issues also come into play, in terms of how clients perceive such projects and interpret AMK's intentions. As a for-profit business, AMK needs to protect its image. A cultural dynamic exists within Cambodia (potentially due to the sheer number of NGOs that arrived to do relief work there in the early 1990s) whereby if clients see something as an 'NGO service', they refuse to pay for it. Huot Sokha (AMK's Chief Business Officer) reflects on this: 'Even a few weeks ago, some clients refused to pay their loans, because they still think of AMK as a Concern charity project.' When we talked to clients at the Bantay Meanchey branch, they still wanted free refreshments at the meeting, and referred to AMK as an 'organization' and to the clients officer as 'teacher', whereas they referred to Acleda (a Cambodian commercial bank) as a 'bank'. The distinction is crucial, especially for an organization in the business of sustaining its operations through profit generation.

AMK still recognizes that its clients face a number of constraints in their lives that prevent them from effectively using financial services. It also recognizes that its huge outreach provides a good platform for leveraging additional services. But it is also clear that its chief role is to provide financial services, and that the principles of scale, sustainability, and client choice are the core drivers of its product offering. So, while non-financial services are regarded as non-core business, and AMK does not provide them directly, it is open to the possibility of referring its clients to other organizations that can meet those needs. Partnerships potentially allow AMK to leverage the specialized skills that a partner company or charity brings to the table, however the lines must be kept clear for clients in terms of organizational identity, and should not require AMK to work differently or affect the client's ability to choose which products they purchase. For example, AMK has come back to water filters, but in a completely different way. This time, it will not try to promote or market the product. Its role will simply be to connect the partner company to AMK's network of clients, and to provide loans that clients can use to purchase the filters. The choice of whether to do so will remain fully with the clients, and AMK will not attempt to influence this. Thus, water filter loans will be treated in the same way as any other loan: they are available, but not obligatory.

The savings story: bringing it all together

AMK's experience with savings neatly pulls together all six insights in this book. It involves understanding clients' needs, responding in an appropriate and innovative way, and building a business model that works within a changing landscape. Not only that, but the path that AMK chose to address the needs of its core poor clients (namely through agent-based mobile savings) made it re-think its entire strategy around its target market, how to balance commercial pressure with the potential social value it could deliver, and how to harness its organizational culture and clarity to keep its focus on poor clients intact.

The backdrop to the story is this: in its early days, AMK's research focused on understanding the opportunities and risks its clients faced, and where financial services might help them address these needs. Credit is, of course, useful for investing in business or agriculture. However, as discussed in Chapter 1, other financial tools are often more appropriate in helping clients meet day-to-day household needs, life-cycle events (marriages, funerals), and unanticipated needs (e.g. serious illness). Broadly speaking, the same holds true for everyone in the world; it's just that the poverty status of a typical microfinance client makes the process of accessing lump sums of cash, at the moment these are required, relatively complicated.

Savings can help clients meet occasional small shortfalls in monthly income, as well as cover larger expenses when they arise. Not only are savings necessary, they're realistic. As we explained in Chapter 1, one of the key 'light-bulb' moments arising from AMK's research in its early years was that (contrary to popular belief), clients were in fact able to save. What they *weren't* able to do was save regularly, or in large amounts, or in ways that were reliably secure (i.e. not subject to loss or depreciation). So the savings story is first and foremost about a 'felt' social need, and about an institution that made several different attempts (not all successful) to respond to that need.

In Chapter 1, we talked about how the Concern programme gave clients access to an internal savings fund, which in theory should have been quite useful, both in meeting clients' needs and in giving them a certain measure of autonomy over their financial affairs. However in light of the inefficiencies for staff involved, and the unclear payoffs (when it wasn't directly managing the fund), AMK removed this feature of its methodology. In 2004, when AMK launched its emergency loan product (in part designed to replace the internal fund, in terms of quick access to lump sums), it also introduced a new voluntary savings product, enabling clients to freely deposit and withdraw small amounts of savings (minimum balance was less than $0.13) from their own personal savings account. To encourage clients to save, the interest rate was set at a very high 18 per cent per annum. On enrolment, each client was given a passbook to record their savings transactions. In theory, transactions could be carried out at either village bank meetings or at AMK branch offices, however given the extreme distance between the two, clients tended to transact at the former.

In theory, this sounded like a great product idea, and it was certainly a favourable interest rate for clients to grow their savings. However, over time, the product saw very limited uptake; indeed, AMK had fewer than 1,800 savings accounts by 2009 (compared with 217,477 borrowers at the same time). Moreover, clients weren't saving very much: in 2009, average savings balances equated to less than one tenth of the average loan size. Why this lukewarm response from clients? The 2008 strategic plan gives us some insights: 'The likely difficulty seems to be in limited access for transactions, since AMK client officers travel only once a month to each village. In such a situation, the general savings becomes a recurring deposit of sorts, with great difficulty for clients in cases where they want to access their account urgently.' That is to say, the product fell down on the need to provide clients with the flexibility they needed to manage their uncertain financial lives. The issue of trust was also important. As Tanmay Chetan (former CEO) wrote in 2007: 'One argument often put forward is that the recent history of Cambodia has resulted in low levels of trust among individuals and from civil society, and as a result, people might not want to risk their savings with private institutions. There is evidence of [widespread] loss of savings during 1995–2002, when many banks were closed and people invariably lost their deposits in these banks.' Getting clients to save was a real challenge not just for AMK, but for other microfinance organizations as well. The reputational damage to financial institutions was not confined to one socio-economic stratum, either. Frances Sinha (SPC and Board member) recalls a conversation with AMK's Chief Operations Officer, Mam Chouem, in 2011. When she asked him if he would trust his savings to a bank, he quickly responded, 'No way!'

New possibilities

That however, is not the end of the savings story. In 2007, AMK considered applying to the National Bank of Cambodia for a banking licence, but ultimately rejected the idea because the capital requirements were too steep, and the institutional requirements in terms of regulatory compliance were too complex for AMK's state of corporate maturity. In 2009, however, the National Bank created a new legal framework for deposit-taking microfinance organizations, with less stringent regulatory requirements. It was one step down from being incorporated as a formal bank, but it did allow holders to take deposits from the general public (not just its existing borrowers) and to offer money transfer services. AMK seized the opportunity; it was one of the first microfinance organizations to apply, and its deposit-taking licence was granted the same year. This moment was a watershed for AMK: it signalled the start of its strategic transformation into a provider of broader microfinance services.

AMK's agent-banking model

AMK established a network of 900 village-based agents, located close to rural clients' homes. These agents are independent people (often running small shops) who are provided with a mobile phone to undertake savings and transfer transactions on behalf of clients. Clients can deposit, withdraw, or transfer money from any agent (or from one of AMK's 130 branches and sub-branches). There is no minimum amount for deposit or withdrawal, and fees are only charged for withdrawals and money transfers.

Agents receive a small commission (between 20 and 50 per cent of the transaction fee) for registering and managing clients, and for processing savings and transfer transactions on behalf of AMK. The agent is required to keep a $50 cash balance (reconciled on a weekly basis with the branch office) and to use this to transact with clients.

Importantly, these new channels allowed AMK to break down the time and distance barriers that had plagued its offering in the past. The previous model, which provided savings services to clients through monthly client officer visits, or at the branches, simply didn't work from a flexibility point of view. Clients valued savings that were accessible when, and where, they needed them. For this reason, AMK created an agent-banking model, which enabled clients to deposit and withdraw their savings in their local area. Agents are often flexible with their working hours as they are members of the local community, and AMK data shows that 20 per cent of transactions take place outside normal office hours (agents are able to access the service from 6 am to 10 pm).

At the time of writing, the agent-banking model has moved from pilot to scale, but it remains a work in progress and is yet to be proven in the market. However, for AMK, the ability to diversify its product offering has come at just the right time: market saturation means fierce competition for clients, and being a market leader in new products is a significant advantage. The ability to offer savings and transfer services to non-clients has meant that AMK's potential savings market has expanded drastically – a critical point in terms of balancing volume with costs.

This story, however, is not about how AMK has found new ways of meeting clients' needs. While providing a service to target clients was AMK's primary motivation, it had an institutional motivation as well: namely the pressing need to reduce the risk of volatility involved in securing foreign loan capital. The savings licence allowed AMK to potentially mobilize large amounts of local currency in the form of savings (which it could on-lend to its clients in the form of credit). This was especially important in light of the global financial crisis: given a general paucity of local investors, microfinance organizations by and large relied on foreign investors (who until that point had been scrambling over each other to invest in the Cambodian microfinance sector) to fund their operations. For most lenders, this debt was delivered (and repaid) in dollars or euros. While many Cambodians use the dollar, AMK's rural clients mostly borrow and repay in Cambodian riel. However, after the financial crisis, foreign investors slowed their lending to Cambodia owing to the losses that some lenders faced in India, leading to stricter country exposure limits. Being able to mobilize local capital (in the form of savings) was not only less risky for microfinance organizations, but potentially less costly in the medium-to-long term (once the infrastructure for savings was in place).

A new way of doing business

If agent-based banking gives clients the flexibility to save when they have the money, and to tap into those savings when needed, and if it is profitable for AMK, then it would seem to be a fairly prototypical win-win scenario. Not so. Making agents really work for clients, and the institution, and indeed the agents themselves, turned out to be a delicate balancing act (one that is still in progress).

First and foremost, the agent model represents a significant departure from business as usual for AMK. Rather than being in control of its products and services through staff it has recruited, trained, and managed itself (and for whom AMK's social mission is at the heart of their work), AMK is now working with external agents who might not be interested in AMK's social value proposition, but rather see savings and money transfer as a pure business opportunity. While AMK might (in the past) have been willing to forsake short-term financial gains in favour of long-term social value, agents may respond to commercial motivations alone. Why does this matter? Because the agent model is challenging, and it takes time to build the volume of transactions that makes the model worthwhile from a business perspective. Working in this way, it's not just about balancing the priorities of the client and the institution: there are now three stakeholder groups in the mix. Today, AMK is still seeking the sweet spot in terms of making savings services accessible to clients while ensuring the business is profitable for AMK and agents alike.

Part of this is about getting the balance right between the supply of agents and the demand for services. After the pilot, AMK scaled back the density of agents, resulting in longer travelling distances for clients, but greater volume and revenue for agents. The other part is in trying to encourage demand. This is where the client wants versus client needs insight (see Chapter 1) comes into focus: responding to both is the only way of pulling a beneficial product through the marketplace. Clients need a savings safety net to cope with risk. AMK is interested in getting clients to save, but recognizes that there's a greater market demand for remittances – both for migrant workers to send money home to their families, and to link Cambodian families (whose members are geographically separated) into a broader real-time financial support network. So the balance to be struck lies in giving sufficient weight to transfer services to get clients through the door, and then, once they're in, encouraging them to save as well.

This story becomes even more interesting when we consider how AMK tried to make agent savings work for it as an organization. If AMK were offering savings simply to serve clients' needs, then all it would have needed to do was create a business model that made savings work financially from a cost perspective. However, looking at savings as a means of mobilizing capital meant that AMK couldn't treat this as a niche product; it had to do savings on a scale that would generate significant income for the organization. So, if scale was the priority, where was the problem? Quite simply, it was AMK's social mission. Every other deposit-taking microfinance organization in Cambodia has used its licence to mobilize relatively large deposits from the urban middle classes, and there's a good reason for this. The business case for providing savings to poor clients (in terms of making it a profitable product) is unclear at best. The volume of savings available from AMK's poor rural target clients simply would not generate the capital needed. Indeed, just getting the operation to break even would be difficult. This presented a major dilemma for AMK and was the focus of much debate at Board level.

If the business model of providing savings to AMK's own clients through agents would not work financially, what would? The new regulation allowed for offering savings services to non-clients; but while serving poor non-clients in the branch areas would build important economies of scale that agents needed, this would still not mobilize the volume of savings that AMK was looking for. Also, from a public perception perspective (as touched upon by Tanmay Chetan earlier), it was doubtful that an agent network alone would attract the level of trust needed to build a savings service at significant scale. In the end, a two-pronged strategy was agreed, with AMK focusing both on agent savings for its core clients (poor people), and savings mobilization from a newly defined secondary target market. That is, AMK decided to begin serving middle-income people, who would save larger amounts, through the branch network. Essentially the agent and branch savings products are the same, but delivered through different channels.

This decision had far-reaching implications, in terms of turning AMK into an organization fit for the purpose of serving middle-income clients. To successfully build a savings product in the market for this secondary group, AMK had not only to upgrade its savings products (introducing, for example, higher interest rates for large deposits, longer-term and fixed-deposit accounts), but to build a level of trust and awareness among this new group to make these products attractive in the market place. Image was everything, especially for middle-income clients coming into the branches to save. This meant a programme of substantial investment in upgrading AMK's physical branch network; if not quite to the standard of the other microfinance organizations lining the streets of every rural town, then at least by building attractive branch offices with glass counters, comfortable chairs, television screens playing marketing videos, and all the usual trappings of a regular (trustworthy) bank branch. Getting the word out to the new secondary market was also important, and this meant a total branding overhaul (with a new logo), a marketing campaign, prize promotions, and attractive interest rates. This investment in branch upgrading, branding and marketing has enhanced AMK's reputation as a bank that can be trusted with savings; and this has had a spillover effect on the agent savings (focused on poorer clients), especially where mobile savings clients have heard about AMK savings through radio advertisements.

However, the effort and investment AMK is directing towards this secondary market carries significant risks in terms of a change of culture and focus for staff. The risk is particularly poignant in light of AMK's past experience with its individual lending product, which became overheated, with a lack of checks and balances in place to keep the focus on poorer clients. Thus, having renewed its focus on its core principles, and really interrogated the intersection of growth with quality, AMK's Management and Board have been very aware of the need to balance its priorities between agent banking and branch banking. In practice, this has meant giving equal weight to both (financially and in terms of management time). In 2013, for example, the Board turned down Management requests to roll out more ATMs (for urban middle-class clients) and asked for a greater focus on the agent roll-out. In truth, however, having embarked on both agent-banking and branch-based savings strategies, the imperative for AMK is to make sure that both work. The idea is not to consider challenges purely in the context of the moment, but to take a long-term view of how things could develop. The core is to get the product right, while recognizing that the delivery channel may evolve. The ATM platform, for example, could be used by both sets of clients, and it may be that in the long term AMK rolls these out into the villages.

Looking ahead

When you step back to consider the stories in this chapter, what emerges is one golden thread: the clarity of purpose that has informed AMK's approach consistently as it has evolved over the years. AMK has seen opportunities and faced challenges, and has made innovative (often radical) choices around what the organization does, and how it does it. Throughout, the golden thread – that key clarity – has been AMK's commitment to understanding and responding to the needs of its core clients, while balancing its response with the imperative to build a viable business.

While there have certainly been innovations, these can be characterized as products of the moment: products of AMK's own capacity, and the opportunities and risks it faces in the marketplace, at the time they are conceived. In this way, some innovations of today will doubtless fade away as new ones emerge. Others will endure. What is certain is that in 10 years' time, AMK is likely to look very different to the AMK of today. So when we encourage other organizations to learn lessons from AMK, we're not talking about adopting the particular solutions AMK's leadership found to a particular challenge. Rather, the real value in this story is the *questions* that it asked to arrive at those solutions. The six insights in this book get to the heart of these questions; questions that are relevant to any organization seeking to apply a social value lens to its business model, and so be more effective in the business of doing good.

Notes

1. See for example Elizabeth Rhyne's article, 'The yin and yang of microfinance: reaching the poor and sustainability', *MicroBanking Bulletin*, July 1998: 6–8.
2. Comparable figures for sustainable South Asian microfinance organizations working at the low end of the market stood at around 200 clients per client officer.
3. Data based on 13 microfinance organizations who partner with Oikocredit.
4. Today, instead of client officers, AMK has specialist savings officers and specialist credit officers.

References

AMK (2014) *AMK Cambodia – Have AMK loans helped its clients improve their over-all wellbeing?* [Change study, available online] <https://www.incofin.com/sites/default/files/attachments/newsitems/Change%20Study_AMK_2014.pdf> (accessed 4 October 2014)

Chetan, T. (2007) *Are Social and Financial Objectives Mutually Exclusive? The experience of AMK, Cambodia.* Small Enterprise Development Journal (18:1), Rugby: Practical Action Publishing, <http://dx.doi.org/10.3362/0957-1329.2007.009> (accessed 4 October 2014)

Conclusions: Taking the road less travelled

On a hot London afternoon, many miles from Cambodia, and many months after we started on this journey, we sit with Kea Borann (CEO) and Tanmay Chetan (Chair of the Board) to discuss their feedback on the first draft of this book. Despite the oppressive heat (now increasingly common in temperate England), there's real lightness and energy to our conversation, as well as a familiarity and ease borne of months of Skype calls, emails, and international travel: hallmarks of a changing and increasingly interconnected world. Our analysis, as external observers, had led us to a place where we felt that the global financial crisis came at just the right time for AMK: the crisis had made it stronger, more resilient, more self-aware. But for us, one question remained: did AMK see things the same way? Had it learned the lessons that the crisis had to offer, and did that mean it wouldn't make the same mistakes again? Borann smiled, and offered up a typically philosophical response: 'To be honest, our business has changed so much in the last two years that we're not likely to face the same challenges again. But, yes, we have become stronger as an organization. Clearer about our purpose and what makes us effective. We are in a better position to face not just the old challenges, but new ones as well.'

The problem with taking the road less travelled is that there is rarely a map to guide us. AMK's journey carried it deep into rural Cambodia, into the poorest communities, and along the path to becoming the largest microfinance organization in the country in terms of client outreach. Its journey involved pioneering work, an evolving business model, significant results, and – yes – missteps. The real value of AMK's missteps, however, has not been in the changes it made to get back on track, but in sparking a process of introspection. As a result, AMK's whole approach and mindset is now more responsive to clients' needs, and focused on how it can address these effectively through a profitable and scalable business model that responds to a changing landscape of opportunities and risks.

Of course it's easy for us as authors to look back on AMK's history and neatly parcel it into themes and insights – we benefit both from distance and hindsight. What is more remarkable is that over the past 11 years, this organization has been reflecting, growing, discussing, and improving in real time, amid the sheer operational pressure of serving hundreds of thousands of poor people on a daily basis. AMK has evolved from a charity-focused microfinance project that was missing opportunities to do good (and creating harm through oversight), into a social enterprise that is clear about its role in the world, what works for its clients, and what it needs to do as a result. The path that it has taken to get there has centred around throwing out myriad assumptions: assumptions around what clients really

http://dx.doi.org/10.3362/9781780448640.005

need; that what an organization says it does is the same as its practice on the ground; that visionary leaders are sufficient; and that it isn't possible to turn ideals around creating social value into a sustainable business proposition. More than that, having found the answers to its questions around how to understand clients' needs, how to best serve them, and how to make it work as a business, AMK didn't assume that those answers would stay the same over time.

This is not to suggest, of course, that AMK is the perfect organization. In reality, whether it is or not is beside the point. We're more interested in the fact that the insights emerging from its work can provide food for thought for other organizations grappling with similar issues, and that its own experience demonstrates a positive evolution. Today, AMK has positioned itself in such a way that the changing world is less of a threat; it is poised to take advantage of opportunities to do more good within the marketplace, and avoid the risk of doing harm. Understanding why it does what it does, building the systems and culture to support this, and seeing its role within the broader ecosystem of organizations, also means that AMK is more resilient. This last point is particularly important, as echoed by Borann, who believes that it's less a matter of not repeating past mistakes, and more about sidestepping the new potential pitfalls present in an increasingly complex landscape.

And what about AMK's clients? Is the changing world also less of a threat for them? We explored in Chapter 6 how competition has created greater choice, and how clients have used this to demand more from microfinance organizations. This has certainly driven improvements in client service and reductions in cost. But what about the risks that clients face? The world is a more volatile place than it was 11 years ago. The financial crisis has passed, and the Cambodian economy has recovered, but there is more dependence than ever on the vagaries of the tourism, garment, and construction industries. Floods are increasingly common, as world weather patterns change, and competition in the financial sector is becoming ever fiercer, as new profit-driven companies enter the market, encouraged by the high returns that Cambodian microfinance organizations have achieved. So, yes, the market has created choice, but the risks for clients are greater than ever before. In this context, the steps AMK takes to understand, protect, and respond to the needs of its clients are even more important than they were in the past: rigorous cash-flow analysis, product innovation to give clients better tools to manage their investments and risks, and seeking solutions for clients who are struggling to meet their debt obligations.

How can we do better at doing good?

We live in a world full of innovation and positive change, yet where there is so much damage and harm, and so many people excluded from the benefits. This is because, all too often, doing good is seen in simplistic terms: the understanding is not there, the connections to the reality of people's lives are not there, good conversations are not happening, and the business models created fail to recognize the complex connections that bind people and profit, and fail to build synergies between the two.

Too often our vision is limited by the assumption that it is *the product* that leads to our desired outcomes. It's true that we need to have good products, but it is in the details of how these are delivered that potential good (or harm) is realized. Too often, also, our vision of what can be achieved is blinkered by conventional wisdom about potential clients and their needs. These work to stymie innovation which might otherwise push the boundaries of what is possible to benefit people.

The insights emerging from AMK's experience demonstrate how a deeper understanding of social value can better harness the innovation and energy of business for good. These insights will resonate with all organizations looking to find their own sweet spot between what their clients need and what the organization needs. Also, while the social value lens apparent from AMK's journey is relevant to profit-orientated businesses, social enterprises, and charities alike, it is relevant to each in different ways.

Opportunities for social enterprises

For social enterprises, it's important to grasp the difference in the relationship (or implicit contract) between the client of a social enterprise and that of a commercial enterprise. When we seek to maximize both social and financial returns, those we serve are both customers and beneficiaries. That is, they are customers with the free will, and the right, to make their own decisions about whether and how to use our products and services, and we must acknowledge that they will make these decisions both rationally and emotionally, just as any consumer in the marketplace. At the same time, a social enterprise's responsibility to avoid harm and create value is a step beyond the usual business relationship, and is more similar to the relationship and responsibility that a charity would assume toward its beneficiaries.

Opportunities for charities

The messages of this book are equally important for charities. The principles are the same: the need to ensure that our work is based on a sound knowledge of clients; effective feedback systems; quality delivery; and a business model that allows us to focus on what we do well, and achieve as much scale as we can. While the business model of most charities does not depend on selling products and services on the market, the relationship with the market is still important. Firstly, charitable funds should be used to address the gaps left by the market, not to subsidize inefficiency (such as AMK's fleet of 4x4 cars). Secondly, charities can also usefully cover gaps left by a profit-driven approach, such as investing in financially risky products which might have high social value – for example, AMK's credit line loan. The insights in this book will help charities to deliver more impact for their money. As a case in point, AMK's transformation from a charity to a business catalysed improvements in the quality of its work, and a drive for efficiency that lowered costs for clients while increasing scale.

AMK's transformation also highlights its changing relationship with clients over time. As it took a more business-like approach, it used market feedback to understand whether clients were prepared to purchase a product (and become repeat customers). Where charities are accountable to (and financially reliant on) donors rather than clients, this direct connection to clients may be weaker. So the key question is, how can charities strengthen these market mechanisms to improve their work?

Opportunities for the commercial sector

For profit-orientated businesses, there's a need to examine the relationship between profit and social value. In short, we need to move beyond the idea that we can do well by doing good, and think more in terms of doing good well. In the commercial world, there is increasing recognition that a narrow focus on short-term profits (and ignoring the impact of business on the lives of clients, their communities, and the wider environment) is not in the longer term interests of the business. This is captured by the concept of 'shared value',[1] which highlights the interconnectedness of business, social, and environmental value, and makes the business case for more client centricity and focus on the bigger picture. The shared value framework tells us that what is good for people, their communities, and the environment, is good for the profitability of the business. Rather than having to be at odds with one another, with the right innovative approach, profit and impact can be mutually reinforcing.

While we acknowledge that doing good may be good for business as well as clients, the extent to which a shared value model can create social value is limited, for two reasons. Firstly, the business strategy may look different when it is driven by the pursuit of profit, rather than by clients' needs. This is because there may be a business model for the latter to work, but it may not be the most profitable. So, where businesses engage with clients' lives (even in positive ways) in order to make a profit, there's a risk that clients' underlying needs remain unmet, and that we miss opportunities for doing *more* good in the world. Of course, knowing our clients is at the heart of building a business that commands loyalty and will succeed in the marketplace. But simply responding to what clients want is not sufficient to ensure that we make a positive contribution in the world. A social value approach leads a business to offer products that clients actually *need* to solve a problem or respond to an opportunity – even when they can't express those needs themselves in market feedback surveys. For example, in the case of pharmaceutical companies, where the focus is on business value rather than social value, the development budget will prioritize cholesterol-lowering statins over new antibiotics or malaria vaccines.

Secondly, a profit-driven model can potentially lead to the exclusion of large sections of the world's population, where a company can't make the business case for serving them. In the case of AMK, a shared value model would not have led to a decision to own the dirt road (see Chapter 5). The question of access is not a small one. Technology, globalization, and economic growth are serving to increase access to new products or services for many. Indeed, the millions of people fighting their way out of poverty are becoming the new consumers driving economic progress in many parts of the world. There is a new and burgeoning low-income market: the so-called '5–10s' – people living on $5–$10 per day. Characterized in a popular business book by C.K. Prahalad as 'the fortune at the bottom of the pyramid', this is a huge group of people often excluded from many of the benefits of society (and access to financial services), who could be reached in a profitable way. Yes, there are lots of low-hanging fruit but in reaching them, are we creating as much social value as we might do?

In the face of increasing inequality and persisting poverty, it seems clear that we cannot rely on the market to solve the world's problems. There are more than 1 billion people around the world who still live in extreme poverty, surviving on less than $1.25 a day. These people often lack the ability to meet their basic needs for food, shelter, water, and education, let alone enjoy new norms such as mobile phones. In this context, technologies such as mobile banking are still an economic luxury. Can we find the commercial business case for serving those people left behind, or do we need to focus on building a business model to start addressing some of these needs through sustainable, socially driven businesses? Shared value might make the market work better for some people, but the market isn't the answer to every problem. Rather, the market is the tool, or the means, and as organizations delivering social value, the challenge is to define our relationship with that market.

AMK's experience shows that there are choices to be made in terms of where we put our energy. Mobile banking may bring huge numbers of financially excluded people into the financial system, but millions will still be left behind. If we are to achieve the new World Bank goal of eliminating extreme poverty by 2030, we need deliberate action. New business models may reach huge numbers of people who were previously excluded, but in many cases the market may not be profitable (at least in the short term). In defining the ways in which we work, we need to prioritize the problems to be addressed, and the solutions to these, and then build a business model to make this work. The key lesson we draw from AMK's work is that, while a focus on clients can be good for business, especially in the longer term, the starting point needs to be a focus on understanding clients, and building solutions to their problems or opportunities, rather than simply looking for market opportunities.

One organization in a big world

As we consider AMK's experience, we see that it also relates to some of the bigger questions that the world is asking. These questions look at the limits of what we can reasonably achieve, how to leverage the impact we *are* able to achieve, and the conditions for scaling our impact across the marketplace.

On limits and leveraging

The concept of microfinance was oversold to the world as a 'cure-all' for global poverty. Yet solutions, even good ones, don't exist in a vacuum – and one solution to cure all problems simply does not exist. The futility of giving a client a loan to invest in a business amid macroeconomic collapse highlights the limitation of microfinance. If we are truly to understand the potential social value that our organizations can deliver, this must be grounded in an understanding of the bigger picture that surrounds us.

That said, when we set out to understand this bigger picture, and identify more and more social needs, we risk falling prey to the temptation to try to do it all: provide business training, marketing support, value chain inputs, insurance, relief support, literacy training ... the list goes on. AMK's experience of branching out into non-financial services with limited scope and outreach provides a cautionary tale about organizational overreach. This is not to suggest that a narrow focus on only doing what you do best is necessarily in the best interest of clients. Yes, we need to build organizations that work and are not undermined by 'jack of all trades' strategies, but if we understand the landscape of needs, and what we are best able to deliver, then we can begin to understand how we can create more value for clients by smart leveraging.

Partnerships offer a key opportunity for delivering more good using the marketplace; but it's also important to recognize the risks or social costs inherent in new opportunities and partnerships, and to constantly bring our decisions back to one key question: what does this mean for the lives and livelihoods of those we are trying to serve?

Technology provides a good example of the pitfalls. It breaks down barriers – of time, of distance, of speed – but how do we avoid the risk that it becomes an end in itself, rather than a tool to support our core business? What are the unintended impacts on the fabric of society, or our relationship with clients? For instance, we hear stories of mobile money providers in Kenya, where migrant labourers use technology to send money to their families back home. For those left behind, there can be a breakdown in social cohesion, as workers no longer need to visit their family to deliver those vital economic resources in person; and when families start to break down, and absent husbands start new families, eventually they stop sending money back home.

The rapidly shifting world challenges organizations to think beyond the boundaries of what 'we do' and see the opportunities where others move into 'our space'. For example, in many countries, mobile phone companies have achieved a scale of outreach in financial services in a timeframe that microfinance organizations can only dream of. Combining the best of both organizations, through partnership, might mean harnessing both the outreach to new clients, and the depth of relationships and understanding needed to enhance benefits for clients. By understanding the bigger picture of why we, as organizations, grasp new opportunities, we position ourselves to harness social value and mitigate potential pitfalls through, for example, providing free airtime to mobile money clients, thereby keeping those social networks intact.

On scaling success

Once we recognize that delivering social value isn't always a win-win scenario, and that we can't always make the business case for our business model, what does taking that model to scale look like? In a changing world, AMK's experience raises some interesting questions about defining the relationship between social value and business value. AMK aimed to build a *business model* to reach the most remote parts of Cambodia in a sustainable way, in line with its mission. From the outset, it knew that it would face trade-offs between poverty outreach and profit levels. However, in the long term, this turned out to be a sound *business strategy* in the commercial sense; and the truth is that no one could have predicted this at the time. This highlights the uncertainties and risks that creating social value involves, and the need to effectively support social enterprises in their endeavours. In practical terms, this might mean a move away from the short-term view of profit that punishes longer term returns as riskier, therefore requiring higher financial return and promoting behaviours that undermine social value and potentially cause harm. We also need to recognize the inherent risks of not understanding and responding to clients' needs, and find ways to account for both social and financial returns, while acknowledging that creating new opportunities for clients may create new opportunities for our business.

Social or impact investors play an important role in this. Patient, flexible capital which is able to take risks, or give more weight to factors other than short-term profit, can encourage the development of business models that focus more on social value. That said, this type of investment attitude is currently rare in the capital markets. The financial backing of Concern, for example, uniquely positioned AMK giving it space to innovate and get the model right. There aren't many funders like this, but perhaps this provides an example of the synergies that can link social enterprises and charities.

Looking forward

As our time with AMK draws to a close, what we will walk away with is a profound appreciation for the way in which applying a social value lens has helped AMK remain focused on the needs of its clients, and build a business model that works – and continues to work in a changing world.

This last point is important, because the world is changing, and fast. AMK's model responded to both market failures and opportunities as they developed. Its model may not be right for other organizations, nor even, in future, for AMK itself. Yet the insights discussed in this book proved fundamental to building a business model which created value for clients, and which was well placed to adapt and be resilient to future challenges. While AMK does not have all the answers, we hope the insights we have garnered will help other social purpose organizations take one more step towards being, and staying, in the business of doing good.

Note

1. A concept developed by Professor Michael E. Porter and Mark R. Kramer; see Porter, M.E. and Kramer, M.R. (2011) 'Creating shared value', *Harvard Business Review*, January-February 2011 <http://hbr.org/2011/01/the-big-idea-creating-shared-value> [accessed 7 October 2014]

Reference

Prahalad, C. K. (2004) *The Fortune at the Bottom of the Pyramid*. Philadelphia: Wharton School Publishing.

Index